MARKETING MANAGEMENT

NAVIGATING THE NEW AGE OF MARKETING MANAGEMENT

DR. SUPRIYA GOUTAM

MR. RAKESH KUMAR PANDEY

ER. SARVESH SINGH

To all the passionate marketers and business visionaries who strive to make a difference in the world through creativity, innovation, and dedication. Your relentless pursuit of excellence and your unwavering commitment to understanding and serving customers inspire us all.

To the mentors, teachers, and industry leaders who have shared their wisdom and experiences, guiding the next generation of marketing professionals to greatness.

And to the curious minds and eager learners who never stop asking questions and seeking knowledge. This book is for you, to support your journey and to fuel your aspirations in the ever-evolving field of marketing management.

Foreword

In an era where markets are more dynamic, competitive, and interconnected than ever before, the discipline of marketing has undergone a profound transformation. The rise of digital technologies, shifts in consumer behavior, and the increasing importance of sustainability have created both challenges and opportunities for marketers worldwide. This book, "Marketing Management," is a testament to the evolving landscape of marketing and serves as a comprehensive guide for navigating this complex environment.

Marketing is no longer confined to the realms of product promotion and sales. It has become a strategic function that drives business growth, fosters innovation, and creates lasting value for customers and society. This book delves into the core principles and cutting-edge strategies that define modern marketing management, offering insights that are both practical and forward-thinking.

With best wishes for your journey in marketing management

Preface

Welcome to the fascinating world of Marketing Management. This book is designed to be your comprehensive guide to understanding the core principles and advanced strategies that drive successful marketing practices in today's dynamic and competitive environment.

In the pages that follow, you will embark on a journey through the fundamental concepts and contemporary trends shaping the field of marketing. Our goal is to equip you with the knowledge and skills necessary to navigate the complexities of marketing management and to inspire you to think creatively and strategically about how to connect with customers, build strong brands, and drive business growth.

Why Marketing Management? Marketing is more than just promoting products or services; it is about creating value for customers and building lasting relationships. In an age where consumer preferences are constantly evolving and technology is transforming the way we engage with the market, effective marketing management is essential for any organization aiming to achieve sustainable success.

Acknowledgements

We extend our heartfelt gratitude to the many contributors who have shared their knowledge and experiences, making this book a rich resource for learning. We also thank the readers who inspire us to continuously explore and expand the horizons of marketing management.

As you embark on this journey through the world of marketing management, we encourage you to approach each chapter with curiosity and an open mind. Embrace the challenges and opportunities that come with understanding and applying marketing principles. We hope this book serves as a valuable companion in your quest to become a skilled and strategic marketing professional.

Prologue

In the realm of business, the heartbeat of any successful enterprise lies in its ability to connect with its audience, understand their needs, and deliver unparalleled value. This dynamic interplay between the market and the enterprise is the essence of marketing management—a field that transcends mere transactional exchanges and delves into the deeper relationships that fuel growth, innovation, and sustainability.

As we venture into the intricacies of marketing management, it becomes evident that the landscape is ever-evolving. The traditional paradigms of marketing have been reshaped by technological advancements, shifting consumer behaviors, and a renewed focus on sustainability. This book is a reflection of this transformation, offering a comprehensive guide to navigating the complexities of the modern marketing landscape.

In the chapters that follow, we will explore the foundational principles that underpin effective marketing management, as well as the cutting-edge strategies that are redefining the field. From the critical role of data in shaping marketing decisions to the importance of building authentic brand narratives, each section provides insights that are both timeless and timely.

Welcome to the journey of marketing mastery.

CHAPTER ONE

INTRODUCTION MARKET

Introduction to Market: Characteristics and Elements

Markets are fundamental to the economy and play a crucial role in the exchange of goods and services. Understanding the characteristics and elements of a market is essential for effective marketing management. Here's an introduction to the key aspects:

Characteristics of a Market

Demand and Supply: A market is characterized by the presence of buyers (demand) and sellers (supply). The interaction between demand and supply determines the market price of goods and services.

Competition: Markets typically have multiple sellers competing to attract buyers. This competition drives innovation, improves quality, and keeps prices in check.

Information Flow: Effective markets rely on the free flow of information between buyers and sellers. This includes information about prices, product features, and availability, which helps in making informed decisions.

Accessibility: Markets should be accessible to all participants. This includes physical accessibility (location) and economic accessibility (affordable prices).

Regulation: Markets operate within a framework of rules and regulations set by governments or regulatory bodies to ensure fair practices and protect the interests of consumers and businesses.

Elements of a Market

Products and Services: The core element of any market is the range of products and services available for exchange. These can be tangible goods, intangible services, or a combination of both.

Price: Price is the amount of money that buyers are willing to pay and sellers are willing to accept for a product or service. It is a crucial factor in determining market dynamics.

Place: This refers to the location where transactions occur. It can be a physical market (e.g., a retail store) or a virtual market (e.g., an e-commerce platform).

Promotion: Promotion includes all activities that communicate the value of a product or service to potential buyers. This can involve advertising, sales promotions, public relations, and direct marketing.

Participants: The market consists of various participants, including consumers, businesses, intermediaries (e.g., wholesalers, retailers), and regulators. Each plays a role in the functioning of the market.

Exchange Mechanism: The process through which transactions occur, including the methods of payment, delivery, and after-sales service. This mechanism ensures that goods and services are exchanged efficiently and effectively.

Conclusion

Understanding the characteristics and elements of a market is crucial for anyone involved in marketing management. It helps in analyzing market behavior, predicting trends, and making informed decisions that can drive business success.

CHAPTER TWO

Marketing

Definition and Evolution of Marketing

Definition: Marketing is the activity, set of institutions, and processes for creating, communicating, delivering, and exchanging offerings that have value for customers, clients, partners, and society at large.

Evolution: Marketing has evolved significantly over time:

- **Production Era:** Focused on mass production and efficiency.
- **Sales Era:** Emphasized aggressive sales techniques.
- **Marketing Concept Era:** Shifted to satisfying customer needs and wants.
- **Societal Marketing Era:** Considered the broader impacts on society and the environment.
- **Digital and Relationship Marketing Era:** Leveraged technology for personalized customer engagement.

Scope and Importance of Marketing

Scope: Marketing encompasses a wide range of activities, including market research, product development, pricing, distribution, promotion, and after-sales service. It spans various industries and sectors, influencing both B2B and B2C markets.

Importance: Effective marketing drives business growth by:

- Identifying and meeting customer needs.
- Enhancing brand awareness and loyalty.
- Increasing sales and revenue.
- Supporting innovation and product development.
- Building and maintaining customer relationships.
- Marketing Concepts and Modern Approaches

Marketing Concepts:

- **Production Concept:** Focus on production efficiency.
- **Product Concept:** Emphasis on product quality and innovation.
- **Selling Concept:** Aggressive sales tactics to drive purchases.
- **Marketing Concept:** Prioritizing customer needs and satisfaction.
- **Societal Marketing Concept:** Balancing company profits, customer satisfaction, and societal well-being.

Modern Approaches:

- **Digital Marketing:** Using online channels to reach and engage customers.
- **Content Marketing:** Creating and sharing valuable content to attract and retain customers.
- **Social Media Marketing:** Leveraging social platforms to build relationships and brand awareness.
- **Inbound Marketing:** Attracting customers through relevant and helpful content.
- **Customer Relationship Management (CRM):** Managing interactions with current and potential customers to improve relationships and drive growth.

Marketing Process and Key Activities
Marketing Process:

- **Market Research:** Understanding customer needs, preferences, and market trends.
- **Market Segmentation:** Dividing the market into distinct groups based on characteristics.
- **Targeting:** Selecting the most viable segments to focus on.
- **Positioning:** Creating a unique image and value proposition in the minds of the target market.
- **Marketing Mix:** Developing and implementing strategies for product, price, place, and promotion.
- **Implementation and Control:** Executing the marketing plan and measuring its effectiveness.

Key Activities:

- **Product Development:** Designing and creating products that meet customer needs.
- **Pricing:** Determining the appropriate price to attract customers and achieve profitability.
- **Distribution:** Ensuring products are available to customers through various channels.
- **Promotion:** Communicating the value of the product to the target audience through advertising, sales promotions, and other methods.

Classification of Markets

- **Consumer Markets:** Individuals and households purchasing goods for personal use.
- **Business Markets:** Organizations buying goods and services for production, resale, or operational needs.
- **Global Markets:** International trade and marketing activities.
- **Non-Profit and Government Markets:** Organizations and government bodies that require marketing strategies for their services and initiatives.

Major Functions of Marketing

- **Market Research:** Gathering and analyzing data to understand market dynamics.
- **Product Development:** Innovating and improving products to meet customer demands.
- **Brand Management:** Building and maintaining a strong brand identity.
- **Sales and Distribution:** Ensuring product availability and driving sales.
- **Advertising and Promotion:** Creating awareness and generating demand.
- **Customer Relationship Management:** Building and nurturing long-term customer relationships.

Marketing Environment

The marketing environment includes all external factors that affect marketing strategies and decisions:

- **Microenvironment:** Customers, competitors, suppliers, intermediaries, and public groups.
- **Macroenvironment:** Demographic, economic, natural, technological, political, and cultural forces.

Marketing Mix and Consumer-Centric Marketing Mix

Marketing Mix: The 4 Ps – Product, Price, Place, and Promotion. Consumer-Centric Marketing Mix: Focuses on creating value for the customer, incorporating the 4 Cs – Customer solution, Cost to the customer, Convenience, and Communication.

Marketing System

The marketing system refers to the network of organizations, individuals, and processes that work together to create, communicate, deliver, and exchange offerings that have value for customers and society. It includes producers, intermediaries, consumers, and various supporting services.

CHAPTER THREE

MARKETING MANAGEMENT

Introduction and Definition

Marketing Management is the art and science of choosing target markets and building profitable relationships with them. It involves creating value for customers and capturing value in return. Essentially, it is the strategic process of analyzing, planning, implementing, and controlling marketing activities to achieve organizational objectives.

Objectives and Characteristics

Objectives:

- **Customer Satisfaction:** Meeting or exceeding customer expectations.
- **Profitability:** Ensuring that marketing activities contribute to the financial health of the organization.
- **Market Share:** Increasing the organization's share of the market.
- **Brand Awareness:** Building and maintaining a strong brand presence.
- **Innovation:** Continuously developing new products and improving existing ones.

Characteristics:

- **Customer-Centric:** Focuses on understanding and meeting the needs of the customers.
- **Dynamic:** Adapts to changes in the market environment.
- **Strategic:** Involves long-term planning and setting objectives.
- **Integrated:** Coordinates various marketing activities to create a unified approach.

- **Data-Driven:** Utilizes data and analytics to make informed decisions.

Scope and Importance

- **Scope:** Marketing Management covers a broad range of activities, including:
- **Market Research:** Gathering and analyzing data to understand market trends and customer needs.
- **Product Development:** Designing products that meet customer expectations.
- **Pricing Strategies:** Setting prices that maximize profitability while remaining competitive.
- **Distribution:** Ensuring products are available to customers through various channels.
- **Promotion:** Communicating the value of the product to the target audience through advertising, sales promotions, public relations, and direct marketing.

Importance:

- **Business Growth:** Drives revenue and growth by attracting and retaining customers.
- **Competitive Advantage:** Helps organizations stand out in a crowded marketplace.
- **Customer Relationships:** Builds and maintains strong relationships with customers.
- **Brand Loyalty:** Enhances customer loyalty through effective marketing strategies.
- **Adaptability:** Enables organizations to adapt to market changes and trends.

Comparison of Sales and Marketing Management
Focus:

- **Sales Management:** Primarily focuses on the direct sale of products and services.
- **Marketing Management:** Focuses on a broader range of activities including market research, product development, branding, and

promotional strategies.

Approach:

- **Sales Management:** Short-term, immediate goals aimed at achieving sales targets.
- **Marketing Management:** Long-term, strategic goals aimed at building brand equity and customer relationships.

Orientation:

- **Sales Management:** Product-oriented, emphasizing the features and benefits of the product.
- **Marketing Management:** Customer-oriented, focusing on meeting customer needs and delivering value.

Activities:

- **Sales Management:** Involves personal selling, sales promotions, and managing the sales force.
- **Marketing Management:** Involves market research, product planning, pricing strategies, distribution, and promotional activities.

Core Functions

- **Market Research:** Collecting and analyzing data to understand market dynamics and customer preferences.
- **Product Development:** Innovating and improving products to meet customer needs.
- **Brand Management:** Building and maintaining a strong brand identity.
- **Pricing Strategy:** Setting prices that optimize profitability and market competitiveness.
- **Distribution Management:** Ensuring products are available to customers through various channels.
- **Promotional Activities:** Communicating the value of the product to the target audience through advertising, sales promotions, public relations, and direct marketing.

- **Customer Relationship Management (CRM):** Building and nurturing long-term relationships with customers.
- **Performance Measurement:** Assessing the effectiveness of marketing strategies and making necessary adjustments.

CHAPTER FOUR

DEMAND FORECASTING

Demand forecasting is a crucial aspect of marketing management, as it helps organizations predict future customer demand for products and services. Accurate demand forecasting enables businesses to make informed decisions about inventory management, production planning, and resource allocation. Here's a comprehensive look at demand forecasting:

Definition

Demand Forecasting: The process of estimating future customer demand for a product or service over a specific period. It involves analyzing historical data, market trends, and other relevant factors to predict future sales.

Importance of Demand Forecasting

- **Inventory Management:** Helps maintain optimal inventory levels, reducing the risk of stockouts and overstocking.
- **Production Planning:** Enables efficient planning of production schedules to meet anticipated demand.
- **Resource Allocation:** Assists in allocating resources effectively, ensuring that labor, materials, and finances are utilized efficiently.
- **Financial Planning:** Supports budgeting and financial planning by providing insights into expected revenue and costs.
- **Customer Satisfaction:** Ensures that products are available when customers need them, improving customer satisfaction and loyalty.
- **Strategic Decision-Making:** Informs strategic decisions such as market entry, product launches, and promotional activities.

Types of Demand Forecasting

Qualitative Forecasting: Relies on expert opinions, market research, and judgmental insights. Common methods include:

- Delphi Method
- Market Research Surveys
- Expert Opinion

Quantitative Forecasting: Uses statistical and mathematical models to analyze historical data and project future demand. Common methods include:

- Time Series Analysis
- Regression Analysis
- Econometric Modeling

Short-Term Forecasting: Focuses on predicting demand for a short period, typically up to one year. Useful for operational and tactical planning.

Long-Term Forecasting: Involves predicting demand for an extended period, often more than one year. Important for strategic planning and capital investment decisions.

Steps in Demand Forecasting

- **Define Objectives:** Clearly outline the purpose and scope of the forecast.
- **Collect Data:** Gather historical sales data, market trends, and relevant economic indicators.
- **Analyze Data:** Use statistical and analytical tools to identify patterns and trends in the data.
- **Select a Forecasting Method:** Choose an appropriate forecasting method based on the data and objectives.
- **Generate the Forecast:** Apply the selected method to generate demand estimates.
- **Validate and Adjust:** Validate the forecast by comparing it with actual sales data and make necessary adjustments.
- **Monitor and Update:** Continuously monitor the accuracy of the forecast and update it as needed to reflect changes in the market.

Challenges in Demand Forecasting

- **Data Quality:** Inaccurate or incomplete data can lead to unreliable forecasts.
- **Market Volatility:** Rapid changes in market conditions can make forecasting difficult.
- **Seasonality:** Seasonal fluctuations can impact demand patterns and complicate forecasting.
- **External Factors:** Economic downturns, technological advancements, and regulatory changes can influence demand.

Conclusion

Demand forecasting is a vital tool for businesses to plan and operate efficiently. By accurately predicting future demand, organizations can optimize their operations, enhance customer satisfaction, and achieve their strategic goals. Whether using qualitative or quantitative methods, the key to successful demand forecasting lies in continuous monitoring and adaptation to changing market conditions.

CHAPTER FIVE

MARKETING ORGANIZATION

Marketing Organization: Roles and Structure

Functions of the Marketing Manager

A Marketing Manager plays a pivotal role in driving the marketing strategies and initiatives within an organization. Here are some key functions:

Market Research: Conducting research to understand market trends, customer needs, and competitive landscape. This involves analyzing data and generating insights to inform marketing strategies.

Strategic Planning: Developing marketing plans and strategies that align with the organization's goals. This includes setting objectives, identifying target markets, and determining the marketing mix (Product, Price, Place, Promotion).

Product Management: Overseeing the development, launch, and lifecycle of products. This involves working closely with product development teams to ensure products meet customer needs and market demands.

Brand Management: Building and maintaining a strong brand identity. This includes creating brand guidelines, managing brand equity, and ensuring consistent brand messaging across all channels.

Advertising and Promotion: Planning and executing advertising and promotional campaigns to increase brand awareness and drive sales. This involves collaborating with creative teams and agencies to develop compelling marketing materials.

Sales Support: Providing support to the sales team by creating sales tools, conducting training sessions, and developing sales strategies. This helps in achieving sales targets and improving overall sales performance.

Digital Marketing: Managing online marketing efforts, including social media, email marketing, search engine optimization (SEO), and pay-per-click (PPC) advertising. This helps in reaching and engaging with the target audience through digital channels.

Customer Relationship Management (CRM): Implementing strategies to build and maintain long-term relationships with customers. This includes managing customer data, handling customer feedback, and enhancing customer satisfaction and loyalty.

Budget Management: Allocating and managing the marketing budget effectively. This involves monitoring expenditures, measuring ROI, and ensuring that marketing activities are cost-effective.

Performance Analysis: Evaluating the effectiveness of marketing campaigns and strategies. This includes tracking key performance indicators (KPIs), generating reports, and making data-driven decisions to optimize future marketing efforts.

Organizational Structure

The organizational structure of a marketing department can vary depending on the size and nature of the company. Here are some common structures:

Functional Structure: In this structure, the marketing department is divided into specific functions such as market research, product management, advertising, sales support, and digital marketing. Each function is headed by a manager who reports to the Marketing Director or Chief Marketing Officer (CMO).

Example:

- Chief Marketing Officer (CMO)
- Market Research Manager
- Product Manager
- Brand Manager
- Advertising Manager
- Digital Marketing Manager
- Sales Support Manager

Product-Based Structure: In companies with diverse product lines, the marketing department may be organized around specific products or product categories. Each product group has its own marketing team

responsible for all marketing activities related to that product.
Example:

- Chief Marketing Officer (CMO)
- Product A Marketing Team
- Market Research
- Product Management
- Advertising
- Digital Marketing
- Product B Marketing Team
- Market Research
- Product Management
- Advertising
- Digital Marketing

Geographic Structure: For companies operating in multiple regions, the marketing department may be organized based on geographic areas. Each region has its own marketing team that tailors strategies to local markets.
Example:

- Chief Marketing Officer (CMO)
- North America Marketing Team
- Europe Marketing Team
- Asia-Pacific Marketing Team
- Middle East & Africa Marketing Team

Matrix Structure: This combines elements of functional and product-based structures. Employees report to both a functional manager and a product or project manager, promoting collaboration across different areas of expertise.
Example:

- Chief Marketing Officer (CMO)
- Functional Managers (e.g., Market Research, Advertising)
- Product Managers (e.g., Product A, Product B)

Conclusion

The functions of a Marketing Manager and the organizational structure of the marketing department are critical to the success of an organization's marketing efforts. By effectively managing marketing activities and aligning them with organizational goals, marketing managers help drive growth, build strong brands, and foster lasting customer relationships.

CHAPTER SIX

AGRICULTURAL MARKETING

Agricultural marketing is a vital component of the agricultural sector, ensuring that farm products reach consumers efficiently and at fair prices. It encompasses a range of activities that facilitate the movement of agricultural goods from the farm to the final consumer. Here's an in-depth look at agricultural marketing:

Importance:

- **Economic Development:** Agricultural marketing plays a vital role in the economic development of a country by ensuring that farmers get fair prices for their produce, which in turn improves their income and standard of living.
- **Efficient Distribution:** It helps in the efficient distribution of agricultural products from producers to consumers, reducing waste and ensuring food security.
- **Market Integration:** Facilitates the integration of various regional markets, leading to a more unified national market.
- **Price Stability:** Contributes to stabilizing prices by balancing supply and demand.
- **Innovation and Technology:** Encourages the adoption of modern technology and farming practices, improving productivity and quality.

Agricultural Marketing in India:

- **Structure:** In India, agricultural marketing includes activities related to the collection, grading, processing, storage, transportation, and distribution of agricultural produce.

- **Mandis:** The Agricultural Produce Market Committee (APMC) Act regulates the operation of wholesale markets, also known as mandis, where farmers sell their produce.
- **eNAM:** The National Agriculture Market (eNAM) is an online trading platform aimed at creating a unified national market for agricultural commodities.

Defects and Remedial Measures:

- **Inadequate Infrastructure:** Poor roads, lack of storage facilities, and insufficient market yards lead to high post-harvest losses.

  - **Remedy:**Invest in improving infrastructure, including roads, storage facilities, and market yards.

- **Middlemen:** The presence of multiple intermediaries reduces the profit margins for farmers.

  - **Remedy:** Promote direct marketing channels like farmer markets, cooperatives, and online platforms.

- **Lack of Standardization:** Inconsistent quality and lack of grading reduce market efficiency.

  - **Remedy:** Implement quality standards and grading systems to ensure uniformity.

- **Limited Market Access:** Small and marginal farmers often have limited access to markets due to lack of information and resources.

  - **Remedy:** Enhance market information systems and provide training and support to farmers.

- **Price Fluctuations:** High volatility in prices affects the income stability of farmers.

- ○ **Remedy:** Introduce price support mechanisms and crop insurance schemes.

Conclusion

Agricultural marketing is essential for the smooth functioning of the agricultural sector and the economy as a whole. By addressing the defects in the current system and implementing robust quality standards like BIS and AGMARK, India can ensure fair prices for farmers, improve market efficiency, and enhance consumer confidence in agricultural products.

CHAPTER SEVEN

QUALITY STANDARDS

Bureau of Indian Standards (BIS):

- **Role:** BIS is the national standards body of India, responsible for the development of technical standards, certification, and quality assurance of products, including agricultural goods.
- **Standards Development:** BIS develops and publishes standards for various agricultural products to ensure quality and safety.
- **Certification:** BIS certification indicates that a product conforms to the relevant Indian standards, enhancing consumer confidence.

AGMARK and AGMARK Certification:

- **AGMARK:** AGMARK is a certification mark for agricultural products in India, managed by the Directorate of Marketing and Inspection, an agency under the Ministry of Agriculture and Farmers Welfare.
- **Certification:** AGMARK certification ensures that agricultural products meet the quality standards set by the government.

Benefits:

- **Consumer Trust:** Provides assurance to consumers about the quality and purity of the products.
- **Market Access:** Helps producers access domestic and international markets by meeting stringent quality requirements.
- **Price Premium:** Certified products often fetch a higher price in the market due to their perceived quality.

Conclusion

Agricultural marketing and quality standards are crucial for the development of the agricultural sector and the overall economy. By addressing the defects in the current system and implementing robust quality standards like BIS and AGMARK, India can ensure fair prices for farmers, improve market efficiency, and enhance consumer confidence in agricultural products.

CHAPTER EIGHT

CONSUMERISM AND RECENT TRENDS IN INDIA

Consumer Protection Act: Needs, Rights, and Responsibilities

The Consumer Protection Act, 2019 is a significant piece of legislation in India aimed at protecting consumer rights and ensuring fair trade practices. Here's an overview of its key aspects:

Needs

- **Transparency:** Consumers need clear and accurate information about products and services to make informed decisions.
- **Fair Practices:** Protection against unfair trade practices, misleading advertisements, and exploitation.
- **Redressal Mechanisms:** Access to efficient and timely redressal mechanisms for grievances and disputes.

Rights

- **Right to Safety:** Protection against goods and services that are hazardous to life and property.
- **Right to Information:** Access to complete information about the quality, quantity, potency, purity, standard, and price of goods or services.
- **Right to Choose:** Freedom to choose from a variety of products at competitive prices.

- **Right to be Heard:** Assurance that consumer interests will receive full and sympathetic consideration in the formulation of government policy.
- **Right to Redress:** Right to seek redress against unfair trade practices or unscrupulous exploitation.
- **Right to Consumer Education:** Access to knowledge and skills needed to make informed decisions about goods and services.

Responsibilities

- **Be Informed:** Consumers should gather all necessary information about a product or service before making a purchase.
- **Be Critical:** Evaluate the quality and suitability of products and services.
- **Be Assertive:** Assert their rights and seek redressal for grievances.
- **Be Ethical:** Engage in fair and ethical consumption practices.
- **Be Environmentally Conscious:** Consider the environmental impact of their consumption choices.

Consumer Protection Act, 2019

- **Central Consumer Protection Authority (CCPA):** Established to promote, protect, and enforce the rights of consumers as a class.
- **Consumer Disputes Redressal Commissions:** District, State, and National Commissions to address consumer complaints and disputes.
- **Product Liability:** Provisions for holding manufacturers, service providers, and sellers accountable for defective products or services.
- **E-Commerce Regulations:** Specific rules for e-commerce entities to ensure transparency and protect consumer interests.

The Consumer Protection Act, 2019, aims to empower consumers and create a more transparent and fair marketplace in India. It provides a robust framework for addressing consumer grievances and promoting ethical business practices.

CHAPTER NINE

CONSUMER BEHAVIOUR

Definition

Consumer Behaviour refers to the study of how individuals, groups, and organizations select, purchase, use, and dispose of goods, services, ideas, or experiences to satisfy their needs and desires. It encompasses the psychological, social, and economic factors that influence consumer decisions and actions.

Nature of Consumer Behaviour

1. **Complex:** Consumer behaviour is influenced by a variety of factors, making it complex and multidimensional. It involves emotional, cognitive, and social processes that drive purchase decisions.
2. **Dynamic:** Consumer behaviour is not static; it changes over time based on new information, experiences, and evolving needs. Companies must continuously adapt to these changes to stay relevant.
3. **Individual and Group:** Consumer behaviour can be studied at both the individual level and group level. Individual behaviour focuses on personal preferences and decision-making processes, while group behaviour examines how social influences and interactions impact decisions.
4. **Interdisciplinary:** The study of consumer behaviour draws on various disciplines, including psychology, sociology, anthropology, and economics. This interdisciplinary approach helps in understanding the myriad factors that influence consumer decisions.
5. **Decision-Making Process:** Consumer behaviour involves a decision-making process that includes problem recognition, information search,

evaluation of alternatives, purchase decision, and post-purchase behaviour.

CHAPTER TEN

MARKETING ETHICS

Marketing Ethics refers to the principles and standards that guide behavior in the world of marketing. It involves making morally sound decisions and conducting business practices that are fair, honest, and respectful to all stakeholders, including consumers, employees, suppliers, competitors, and the broader community.

Key Principles of Marketing Ethics

1. **Honesty and Transparency:**

   - Marketers should provide clear, truthful, and accurate information about their products and services.
   - Avoid misleading advertisements, false claims, and deceptive practices that can misinform consumers.

2. **Fairness and Respect:**

   - Treat all customers and stakeholders with fairness and respect, ensuring that marketing practices do not exploit vulnerable groups.
   - Ensure equitable access to products and services without discrimination.

3. **Social Responsibility:**

   - Consider the broader impact of marketing activities on society and the environment.
   - Promote sustainable practices and support social causes that contribute to the well-being of communities.

4. **Consumer Privacy:**

   - Protect consumer data and privacy by adhering to data protection laws and regulations.
   - Obtain consent before collecting personal information and ensure that data is used responsibly.

5. **Product Safety:**

   - Ensure that products and services are safe for consumer use and comply with relevant safety standards.
   - Provide clear instructions and warnings to help consumers use products safely.

Ethical Issues in Marketing

1. **False Advertising:**

   - Making exaggerated or unsubstantiated claims about a product's benefits or features.
   - Ethical marketing requires providing honest and accurate information.

2. **Exploitation of Vulnerable Groups:**

   - Targeting marketing campaigns at vulnerable populations, such as children or the elderly, in a manipulative manner.
   - Ethical marketers should avoid exploiting the weaknesses of these groups.

3. **Greenwashing:**

   - Misleading consumers about the environmental benefits of a product or service.
   - Ethical marketing involves genuine efforts to promote sustainability, not just superficial claims.

4. **Price Gouging:**

- Charging excessively high prices during emergencies or shortages.
- Ethical pricing strategies should reflect fairness and consideration for consumers' financial constraints.

5. **Invasion of Privacy:**

- Collecting and using consumer data without proper consent or transparency.
- Ethical marketers respect consumer privacy and use data responsibly.

Benefits of Ethical Marketing

1. **Builds Trust and Loyalty:**

- Consumers are more likely to trust and remain loyal to brands that demonstrate ethical behavior.
- Ethical marketing fosters long-term relationships with customers.

2. **Enhances Brand Reputation:**

- A reputation for ethical practices enhances the brand image and differentiates the company from competitors.
- Positive word-of-mouth and goodwill can attract more customers.

3. **Reduces Legal Risks:**

- Adhering to ethical standards helps companies comply with laws and regulations, reducing the risk of legal issues and penalties.
- Ethical practices create a safer business environment.

4. **Attracts Ethical Consumers:**

- Growing awareness and concern for ethical practices among consumers mean that ethical brands can attract a larger, more conscientious customer base.
- Ethical consumers are willing to pay a premium for products and services from socially responsible companies.

Conclusion

Marketing ethics is essential for building a sustainable and successful business. By adhering to ethical principles, companies can foster trust, loyalty, and a positive brand image while contributing to the well-being of society. Ethical marketing is not just about compliance but about making a commitment to doing the right thing for all stakeholders.

CHAPTER ELEVEN

MARKET SEGMENTATION

Market Segmentation: Types and Steps

Market segmentation is a crucial process in marketing management, where a broad market is divided into smaller, more manageable segments based on specific criteria. This helps businesses tailor their marketing efforts to better meet the needs and preferences of different customer groups.

Types of Market Segmentation
Demographic Segmentation:

- **Age:** Different age groups have varying needs and preferences.
- **Gender:** Male and female consumers may have different buying behaviors.
- **Income:** Income levels can influence purchasing power and product preferences.
- **Education:** Education level can impact the type of products and services consumers seek.
- **Occupation:** Different occupations may have unique needs and interests.

Geographic Segmentation:

- **Region:** Dividing the market based on geographical regions (e.g., North, South, East, West).
- **Climate:** Differentiating based on climate (e.g., cold, hot, humid) can influence product needs.

- **Population Density:** Urban, suburban, and rural areas may have different consumption patterns.

Psychographic Segmentation:

- **Lifestyle:** Grouping consumers based on their lifestyles and interests.
- **Personality:** Different personality traits can influence purchasing decisions.
- **Values and Beliefs:** Consumers' values and beliefs can impact their buying behavior.

Behavioral Segmentation:

- **Purchase Occasion:** Differentiating based on when consumers buy (e.g., holidays, birthdays).
- **Benefits Sought:** Grouping consumers based on the benefits they seek from a product.
- **User Status:** Segmentation based on user status (e.g., non-users, potential users, first-time users, regular users).
- **Usage Rate:** Categorizing consumers based on their usage rate (e.g., light, medium, heavy users).
- **Loyalty Status:** Grouping consumers based on their loyalty to the brand (e.g., loyal, switchers, non-loyal).

Steps in Market Segmentation

1. **Identify the Market:**

   - Start by defining the broad market you want to segment. This could be based on the industry, product category, or overall customer base.

2. **Determine Segmentation Criteria:**

   - Choose the appropriate criteria for segmenting the market. This could be demographic, geographic, psychographic, behavioral, or a combination of these.

3. **Collect and Analyze Data:**

- ◦ Gather relevant data on the identified criteria. Use market research methods such as surveys, focus groups, and customer data analysis to understand the market better.

4. **Segment the Market:**

- ◦ Divide the market into distinct segments based on the chosen criteria. Each segment should be unique and have specific characteristics that differentiate it from others.

5. **Evaluate and Select Target Segments:**

- ◦ Assess the attractiveness of each segment based on factors such as size, growth potential, profitability, and alignment with your business objectives. Select the segments that you want to target.

6. **Develop Segment Profiles:**

- ◦ Create detailed profiles for each target segment. This includes demographic information, preferences, behaviors, and needs. These profiles help in understanding and addressing each segment effectively.

7. **Design Marketing Strategies:**

- ◦ Tailor marketing strategies to meet the needs and preferences of each target segment. This includes product development, pricing, distribution, and promotional strategies.

8. **Implement and Monitor:**

- ◦ Implement the marketing strategies and continuously monitor their effectiveness. Collect feedback and make necessary adjustments to improve performance and better serve the target segments.

Conclusion

Market segmentation allows businesses to understand and meet the diverse needs of their customers more effectively. By dividing the market into smaller segments and tailoring marketing strategies to each segment, companies can enhance customer satisfaction, increase market share, and achieve better business outcomes.

CHAPTER TWELVE

CUSTOMER RELATIONSHIP MARKETING

Customer Relationship Marketing (CRM) focuses on building and maintaining long-term relationships with customers to foster loyalty and retention. This approach emphasizes understanding customer needs, providing personalized experiences, and creating value beyond just the initial transaction.

Strategies for Customer Relationship Marketing

1. **Personalization:**

   - Tailor communications, products, and services to meet individual customer preferences and needs. Use data and analytics to create personalized experiences.
   - **Examples:** Personalized email campaigns, product recommendations based on past purchases, and customized loyalty programs.

2. **Customer Segmentation:**

   - Divide your customer base into segments based on demographics, behavior, and preferences. Develop targeted marketing strategies for each segment.
   - **Examples:** Segmenting customers by purchase frequency, geographic location, or interests.

3. **Customer Engagement:**

   ◦ Foster continuous interaction with customers through multiple channels, such as social media, email, and mobile apps. Engage customers with relevant content, offers, and updates.
   ◦ **Examples:** Running interactive social media campaigns, hosting webinars, and sending personalized newsletters.

4. **Loyalty Programs:**

   ◦ Implement loyalty programs to reward repeat customers and encourage long-term engagement. Offer incentives such as discounts, exclusive access, and special promotions.
   ◦ **Examples:** Points-based loyalty programs, tiered membership levels, and referral bonuses.

5. **Customer Feedback and Surveys:**

   ◦ Collect feedback from customers to understand their experiences and identify areas for improvement. Use surveys, reviews, and feedback forms to gather insights.
   ◦ **Examples:** Post-purchase surveys, online reviews, and customer satisfaction questionnaires.

6. **Customer Service Excellence:**

   ◦ Provide exceptional customer service at every touchpoint. Ensure that customer inquiries and issues are addressed promptly and effectively.
   ◦ **Examples:** 24/7 customer support, dedicated account managers, and proactive communication.

7. **Relationship Building Activities:**

   ◦ Organize events, webinars, and community activities that allow customers to connect with the brand and each other.
   ◦ **Examples:** Exclusive events for top customers, online forums, and user group meetings.

8. **Omni-Channel Presence:**

   - Maintain a consistent and seamless customer experience across all channels, including online, in-store, and mobile. Ensure that customers can interact with the brand in their preferred way.
   - **Examples:** Integrated CRM systems, unified customer profiles, and synchronized marketing messages.

9. **Content Marketing:**

   - Create and share valuable content that resonates with your target audience. Use blogs, videos, infographics, and social media posts to provide useful information and build trust.
   - **Examples:** Educational blog posts, how-to videos, and industry insights.

10. **Predictive Analytics:**

   - Use data analytics to predict customer behavior and preferences. Anticipate customer needs and proactively offer solutions.
   - **Examples:** Predictive product recommendations, personalized marketing campaigns, and inventory management based on demand forecasts.

Benefits of Customer Relationship Marketing

1. **Increased Customer Loyalty:**

   - Building strong relationships with customers leads to higher loyalty and repeat business. Loyal customers are more likely to choose your brand over competitors.

2. **Enhanced Customer Satisfaction:**

   - Personalized experiences and excellent customer service contribute to higher customer satisfaction. Satisfied customers are more likely to recommend your brand to others.

3. **Higher Lifetime Value:**

   - By nurturing long-term relationships, businesses can increase the lifetime value of customers. Loyal customers tend to spend more over time and generate higher revenue.

4. **Improved Brand Reputation:**

   - Positive relationships with customers enhance the brand's reputation and credibility. Word-of-mouth referrals and positive reviews contribute to a strong brand image.

5. **Cost Savings:**

   - Retaining existing customers is more cost-effective than acquiring new ones. Effective CRM strategies reduce customer churn and lower marketing and sales costs.

6. **Better Insights and Data:**

   - CRM systems provide valuable data and insights into customer behavior and preferences. This information helps businesses make informed decisions and tailor their marketing efforts.

7. **Competitive Advantage:**

   - Strong customer relationships can serve as a competitive advantage, differentiating your brand in the market. Loyal customers are less likely to switch to competitors.

8. **Increased Sales:**

   - Personalized marketing and targeted promotions can drive higher sales and conversion rates. Engaged customers are more likely to respond positively to offers and recommendations.

Conclusion

Customer Relationship Marketing is a powerful approach to building lasting relationships with customers, enhancing satisfaction, and driving business growth. By implementing effective CRM strategies and focusing on customer-centric practices, businesses can achieve long-term success and a loyal customer base.

CHAPTER THIRTEEN

MARKETING INFORMATION SYSTEM (MIS)

Definition

A **Marketing Information System (MIS)** is a structured arrangement of data collection, storage, processing, and analysis designed to support marketing decision-making processes. It integrates and organizes information from various sources to provide timely, relevant, and accurate insights that help marketing managers plan, implement, and control marketing activities effectively.

Advantages of MIS

1. **Improved Decision-Making:** By providing accurate and up-to-date information, MIS enables marketing managers to make informed decisions. This reduces uncertainty and enhances the overall effectiveness of marketing strategies.
2. **Efficiency and Productivity:** Automating data collection and analysis streamlines marketing processes, saving time and resources. This leads to higher efficiency and productivity in marketing operations.
3. **Enhanced Market Understanding:** MIS helps in understanding market trends, customer behavior, and competitive dynamics. This insight allows companies to anticipate changes and respond proactively.
4. **Better Customer Insights:** By analyzing customer data, MIS provides valuable insights into customer preferences, needs, and behaviors. This enables personalized marketing and improves customer satisfaction.

5. **Coordination and Integration:** MIS fosters better coordination and integration of marketing activities by providing a unified view of marketing data. This ensures that all marketing functions work towards common goals.
6. **Performance Monitoring:** MIS allows companies to track the performance of marketing campaigns, measure ROI, and identify areas for improvement. This continuous monitoring helps in optimizing marketing efforts.

Components of MIS

1. **Internal Records:** Data collected from within the organization, including sales records, customer data, inventory levels, and financial information. These records provide a historical perspective and help in analyzing trends and patterns.
2. **Marketing Intelligence:** Information gathered from external sources such as market research, competitor analysis, industry reports, and public databases. This component helps in understanding the broader market environment and identifying opportunities and threats.
3. **Marketing Research:** Systematic collection and analysis of data specific to a particular marketing problem or opportunity. This includes surveys, focus groups, experiments, and observational studies that provide detailed insights into consumer behavior and preferences.
4. **Analytical Tools:** Techniques and software used to process and analyze data, such as statistical analysis, data mining, and predictive modeling. These tools help in converting raw data into actionable insights.
5. **Decision-Support Systems (DSS):** Interactive software applications that assist marketing managers in decision-making by providing simulations, what-if analyses, and scenario planning. DSS tools help in evaluating different marketing strategies and their potential outcomes.
6. **Customer Relationship Management (CRM) Systems:** Integrated systems that manage interactions with customers, store customer data, and facilitate personalized marketing efforts. CRM systems are essential for building and maintaining strong customer relationships.

Achieving Organizational Objectives with MIS

1. **Strategic Planning:** MIS provides the data and insights needed for strategic planning. By understanding market trends, customer preferences, and competitive dynamics, companies can develop effective marketing strategies that align with organizational goals.
2. **Market Segmentation:** With detailed customer data, MIS helps in identifying distinct market segments and tailoring marketing efforts to meet the specific needs of each segment. This leads to more targeted and effective marketing campaigns.
3. **Product Development:** MIS provides insights into customer needs and preferences, guiding the development of new products and services that meet market demands. This ensures that product offerings remain relevant and competitive.
4. **Pricing Strategies:** By analyzing market data, customer behavior, and competitor pricing, MIS helps in setting optimal prices for products and services. This maximizes profitability while remaining competitive.
5. **Promotional Effectiveness:** MIS tracks the performance of marketing campaigns and measures their impact on sales and customer engagement. This allows companies to optimize promotional strategies and allocate resources more effectively.
6. **Customer Retention:** With CRM systems integrated into MIS, companies can manage customer relationships more effectively, improving customer satisfaction and retention. Personalized marketing efforts and responsive customer service enhance loyalty and long-term value.

Conclusion

A well-implemented Marketing Information System is a powerful tool that supports informed decision-making, improves efficiency, and drives business growth. By leveraging the components of MIS, organizations can achieve their marketing objectives, enhance customer satisfaction, and maintain a competitive edge in the market.

CHAPTER FOURTEEN

Marketing Mix: Product

Definition

The Product in the marketing mix refers to the goods or services that a company offers to its target market. It encompasses everything from design and features to branding and packaging. The product is the cornerstone of a company's marketing strategy, as it must meet the needs and desires of the customer.

Characteristics of a Product

Quality: The standard of the product as measured against similar products. Quality can determine the product's durability, reliability, and performance.

Features: Specific attributes or functionalities that set the product apart from competitors. These could include size, color, materials, or unique capabilities.

Design: The aesthetic and functional aspects of the product. Good design enhances usability and appeal.

Branding: The use of a name, term, symbol, or design to identify and differentiate a product from others. Strong branding creates recognition and loyalty.

Packaging: The process of designing and producing the container or wrapper for a product. Packaging serves to protect the product, provide information, and enhance its appearance.

Labeling: Providing information about the product on its packaging. Labels include details such as ingredients, usage instructions, and legal requirements.

Support Services: Additional services offered with the product, such as warranties, customer service, and technical support.

Product Lifecycle: The stages a product goes through from development to decline – introduction, growth, maturity, and decline.

Types of Products

1. Consumer Goods:

- **Convenience Products:** Items that are purchased frequently and with minimal effort, such as snacks, toiletries, and cleaning supplies.
- **Shopping Products:** Goods that are bought less frequently and compared on attributes like quality, price, and style, such as electronics, clothing, and furniture.
- **Specialty Products:** Unique items with specific characteristics that consumers will make a special effort to purchase, such as luxury cars, designer clothing, and high-end electronics.
- **Unsought Products:** Goods that consumers do not actively seek out and often require marketing efforts to be sold, such as life insurance, funeral services, and emergency repairs.

2. Industrial Goods:

- **Raw Materials:** Basic materials that are processed into final products, such as minerals, chemicals, and agricultural products.
- **Component Parts:** Items that are used in the production of other goods, such as automobile parts, computer chips, and machinery components.
- **Capital Goods:** Durable items used in the production of other goods and services, such as buildings, machinery, and equipment.
- **Supplies and Services:** Consumables and services used in the day-to-day operations of a business, such as office supplies, maintenance services, and utilities.

Services as Products

Services are intangible products that cannot be physically owned or stored. They are consumed at the point of delivery and often involve direct interaction between the service provider and the customer. Key characteristics of services include:

1. **Intangibility:** Services cannot be seen, touched, or possessed. They are experiences or actions.
2. **Inseparability:** Services are produced and consumed simultaneously. The quality of the service depends on the interaction between the provider and the consumer.
3. **Variability:** The quality of services can vary based on who provides them, when, where, and how they are delivered.
4. **Perishability:** Services cannot be stored for later use. Once delivered, they cannot be returned or resold.
5. **Ownership:** Services do not result in ownership. Customers pay for access or use, not ownership.

Types of Services:

- **Professional Services:** Expertise-based services such as consulting, legal, and medical services.
- **Business Services:** Services that support business operations, such as IT support, marketing, and logistics.
- **Personal Services:** Services provided to individuals, such as haircuts, fitness training, and education.
- **Public Services:** Services provided by the government or non-profit organizations, such as healthcare, education, and public safety.

Conclusion

The product element of the marketing mix encompasses a wide range of goods and services designed to meet customer needs. Understanding the characteristics and types of products and services allows businesses to create offerings that resonate with their target market, driving customer satisfaction and business success.

CHAPTER FIFTEEN

PRODUCT PLANNING

Product Planning: A Comprehensive Guide
Process, Development, and Benefits

Product Planning is a critical aspect of marketing management that involves creating and managing a product throughout its lifecycle. It ensures that a product meets market needs and achieves organizational goals.

Process:

1. **Idea Generation:** This is the initial phase where new product ideas are generated through various sources such as market research, customer feedback, competitor analysis, and brainstorming sessions.
2. **Idea Screening:** Evaluate the generated ideas to identify those with the highest potential. Assess feasibility, market demand, and alignment with organizational goals.
3. **Concept Development and Testing:** Develop detailed concepts for the selected ideas and test them with target customers to gather feedback and refine the concepts.
4. **Business Analysis:** Conduct a thorough analysis of the product's potential market size, costs, pricing, and profitability. Determine the financial viability of the product.
5. **Product Development:** Create prototypes or samples of the product. This phase involves design, engineering, and development to bring the product concept to life.
6. **Market Testing:** Introduce the product to a limited market to assess consumer response and identify any issues before a full-scale launch.
7. **Commercialization:** Launch the product in the market with a comprehensive marketing plan. This includes production, distribution, and promotional activities.

8. **Post-Launch Review:** Monitor the product's performance and gather feedback to make necessary adjustments and improvements.

Development:

- Involves collaboration between different departments, including R&D, marketing, finance, and production.
- Requires continuous monitoring and iteration based on market feedback and changing trends.

Benefits:

1. **Meeting Customer Needs:** Ensures that products are designed to meet customer requirements and preferences, leading to higher satisfaction and loyalty.
2. **Competitive Advantage:** Helps in developing innovative products that differentiate the company from competitors.
3. **Efficient Resource Allocation:** Enables better planning and allocation of resources, reducing waste and improving efficiency.
4. **Risk Mitigation:** Identifies potential issues early in the development process, allowing for timely corrections and reducing the risk of failure.
5. **Revenue Growth:** Supports the introduction of new products that can generate additional revenue streams and drive business growth.

Product Mix and Adjustment/Modification
Product Mix:

- The product mix, also known as the product assortment, refers to the complete range of products offered by a company. It includes all product lines and individual products within those lines.

Adjustment/Modification:

1. **Product Line Extension:** Adding new products to an existing product line to cater to different customer segments or needs.
2. **Product Line Contraction:** Removing unprofitable or less popular products from the product line to focus on more successful items.

3. **Product Modification:** Making changes to existing products to improve their features, quality, or performance. This can include updates, redesigns, or enhancements.
4. **Product Repositioning:** Changing the target market or product perception to better meet customer needs or adapt to market changes.

Benefits:

- Keeps the product portfolio relevant and aligned with market trends.
- Addresses changing customer preferences and technological advancements.
- Improves overall profitability and market share by focusing on successful products.

Product Positioning and Repositioning
Product Positioning:

- The process of creating a unique image and identity for a product in the minds of the target customers. It involves defining the product's key benefits, differentiating features, and competitive advantages.

Steps in Product Positioning:

1. **Identify Target Market:** Understand the specific needs and preferences of the target market.
2. **Analyze Competitors:** Evaluate competitor products and their positioning strategies.
3. **Define Unique Selling Proposition (USP):** Determine the key benefits and features that make the product stand out.
4. **Create Positioning Statement:** Develop a clear and concise statement that communicates the product's value proposition to the target market.
5. **Implement Positioning Strategy:** Integrate the positioning statement into marketing communications, branding, and promotional activities.

Product Repositioning:

- The process of changing the product's positioning to adapt to new market conditions, target a different audience, or address changing customer preferences.

Reasons for Repositioning:

- Market saturation or declining sales.
- Changes in consumer preferences or market trends.
- Competitive pressure or new entrants.
- Product upgrades or improvements.

Steps in Product Repositioning:

1. **Market Research:** Conduct research to understand the reasons for repositioning and identify new opportunities.
2. **Redefine Target Market:** Identify the new target market and their needs.
3. **Revise Positioning Statement:** Develop a new positioning statement that reflects the updated value proposition.
4. **Adjust Marketing Mix:** Modify the product, pricing, distribution, and promotional strategies to align with the new positioning.
5. **Communicate Changes:** Effectively communicate the repositioning to the target market through various marketing channels.

Benefits of Repositioning:

- Revitalizes the product and increases its appeal to a new or broader audience.
- Enhances competitive advantage and market relevance.
- Addresses changing market dynamics and consumer preferences.

Conclusion

Product planning, development, and management are essential for creating successful products that meet customer needs and drive business growth. By effectively managing the product mix, positioning, and repositioning strategies, companies can ensure that their products remain competitive and relevant in the market.

PRODUCT DEVELOPMENT

Product Development is the process of creating a new product or improving an existing one to meet customer needs and market demands. It involves a series of steps that transform a product concept into a market-ready solution. Effective product development is crucial for maintaining competitiveness and driving business growth.

Steps in Product Development

1. **Idea Generation:**

   - **Sources:** Ideas can come from various sources, including market research, customer feedback, employees, competitors, and new technologies.
   - **Brainstorming:** Encourage creative thinking and open discussions to generate a wide range of ideas.

2. **Idea Screening:**

   - **Evaluation:** Assess the feasibility, potential, and alignment with company goals of each idea.
   - **Selection:** Choose the most promising ideas for further development while discarding those that do not meet the criteria.

3. **Concept Development and Testing:**

- **Concept Development:** Create detailed descriptions, sketches, and prototypes of the selected ideas.
- **Testing:** Present the concepts to target customers and gather feedback to refine the product idea.

4. **Business Analysis:**

- **Market Analysis:** Evaluate the target market size, growth potential, and competitive landscape.
- **Financial Analysis:** Estimate costs, revenue, and profitability. Assess the financial viability of the product.

5. **Product Development:**

- **Design and Engineering:** Develop detailed designs, specifications, and engineering plans. Create prototypes or samples.
- **Testing:** Conduct rigorous testing to ensure the product meets quality, safety, and performance standards.

6. **Market Testing:**

- **Pilot Launch:** Introduce the product to a limited market or test group to gauge customer response and identify any issues.
- **Feedback and Adjustment:** Collect feedback from the test market and make necessary adjustments to the product.

7. **Commercialization:**

- **Launch Plan:** Develop a comprehensive launch plan, including marketing, distribution, and sales strategies.
- **Production:** Ramp up production to meet anticipated demand.
- **Distribution:** Ensure the product is available in the right channels to reach the target customers.
- **Promotion:** Implement promotional activities to create awareness and drive initial sales.

8. **Post-Launch Evaluation:**

- **Monitoring:** Track product performance, sales, and customer feedback.
- **Continuous Improvement:** Make ongoing improvements based on customer insights and market trends.

Benefits of Effective Product Development

1. **Meeting Customer Needs:** Ensures that products are designed to address customer preferences and solve their problems, leading to higher satisfaction and loyalty.
2. **Competitive Advantage:** Helps in creating innovative products that differentiate the company from competitors.
3. **Revenue Growth:** Supports the introduction of new products that can generate additional revenue streams and drive business growth.
4. **Adaptability:** Allows companies to respond quickly to market changes and emerging trends.
5. **Brand Strength:** Enhances the brand's reputation and credibility by consistently delivering high-quality and innovative products.
6. **Market Expansion:** Enables companies to enter new markets and attract new customer segments.

Conclusion

Product development is a multifaceted process that requires careful planning, collaboration, and execution. By following a structured approach, companies can create products that meet market demands, drive growth, and maintain a competitive edge.

CHAPTER SEVENTEEN

PRODUCT LINE

Product Line: Product Line and Extension

Product Line

A Product Line is a group of related products offered by a company that serve a similar function, are marketed together, or appeal to the same customer group. These products often share certain characteristics, such as similar technology, branding, or distribution channels.

Examples:

- **Automobile Industry:** A car manufacturer may have a product line consisting of sedans, SUVs, and trucks.
- **Cosmetics Industry:** A beauty brand may offer a product line of skincare products, including cleansers, moisturizers, and serums.

Product Line Extension

Product Line Extension is the practice of expanding an existing product line by adding new variants, such as new flavors, sizes, colors, or forms. This strategy aims to cater to different customer preferences and market segments while leveraging the existing brand's strength.

Examples:

- **Food and Beverage Industry:** A soft drink company might introduce new flavors to its existing line of beverages.
- **Technology Industry:** A smartphone manufacturer may release new models with different features and price points under the same brand.

Types of Product Line Extensions:

1. **Horizontal Line Extension:** Introducing new products at the same price and quality level as existing products to appeal to different tastes. Example: Different flavors of a snack.
2. **Vertical Line Extension:** Adding products that vary in price, quality, or performance to target different market segments. Example: A car brand introducing luxury and budget-friendly models.

Merits of Product Line and Extension

1. **Market Expansion:**

   - **Benefit:** Allows a company to reach new customer segments and expand its market share.
   - **Example:** A skincare brand introducing a line of products for sensitive skin can attract customers who may not have previously considered the brand.

2. **Economies of Scale:**

   - **Benefit:** Leveraging existing production facilities, distribution channels, and marketing efforts reduces costs.
   - **Example:** A beverage company can produce new flavors using the same manufacturing processes and distribution networks as its existing products.

3. **Brand Loyalty:**

   - **Benefit:** Strengthens customer loyalty by offering a wider range of choices under a trusted brand.
   - **Example:** A technology company with a loyal customer base can introduce new gadgets or accessories that customers are more likely to purchase.

4. **Risk Diversification:**

   - **Benefit:** Diversifying the product line reduces reliance on a single product, spreading risk across multiple products.

- ◦ **Example:** A toy manufacturer introducing different types of toys (e.g., educational, action figures) can mitigate the impact of declining demand for a specific category.

5. **Increased Sales:**

   - ◦ **Benefit:** New products can boost overall sales by attracting new customers and encouraging repeat purchases.
   - ◦ **Example:** A bakery adding gluten-free options to its product line can attract health-conscious consumers and increase sales.

6. **Competitive Advantage:**

   - ◦ **Benefit:** Staying ahead of competitors by continuously innovating and introducing new products.
   - ◦ **Example:** A fashion brand regularly updating its clothing line with new trends can maintain its competitive edge.

7. **Customer Satisfaction:**

   - ◦ **Benefit:** Offering a variety of options enhances customer satisfaction by meeting diverse needs and preferences.
   - ◦ **Example:** An electronics brand offering different sizes and specifications of laptops can cater to various customer requirements.

Conclusion

Expanding a product line through extensions offers numerous advantages, from reaching new customer segments to increasing sales and building brand loyalty. By effectively managing product lines and extensions, companies can enhance their market presence, reduce risks, and meet the evolving needs of their customers.

CHAPTER EIGHTEEN

PRODUCT LIFE CYCLE

Product Life Cycle (PLC)

Importance and Extension

Product Life Cycle (PLC) refers to the stages a product goes through from its introduction to the market until its decline and eventual withdrawal. Understanding the PLC is crucial for effective marketing and product management strategies.

Stages of the Product Life Cycle:

1. **Introduction:** The product is launched, and initial marketing efforts aim to create awareness and stimulate demand. Sales growth is typically slow, and profits may be negative due to high costs.
2. **Growth:** The product gains acceptance, and sales increase rapidly. Marketing efforts focus on differentiation and expanding market share. Profits begin to rise as economies of scale are achieved.
3. **Maturity:** Sales growth slows as the product reaches peak market penetration. Competition intensifies, and marketing strategies emphasize defending market share and extending the product's life. Profits may stabilize or decline.
4. **Decline:** Sales and profits decline as the product becomes outdated or less relevant. Companies may reduce marketing efforts and consider discontinuing the product or finding ways to revitalize it.

Importance of PLC:

1. **Strategic Planning:** Understanding the PLC helps companies develop appropriate marketing strategies for each stage, ensuring effective resource allocation and maximizing profitability.

2. **Market Analysis:** Analyzing the PLC provides insights into market trends, consumer behavior, and competitive dynamics, helping businesses anticipate changes and adapt proactively.
3. **Product Management:** PLC analysis aids in managing the product portfolio, identifying opportunities for new product development, and making informed decisions about product modifications or discontinuations.
4. **Pricing Strategies:** Companies can adjust pricing strategies based on the product's life cycle stage, such as introductory pricing during the launch or discounting during the decline stage.
5. **Promotion and Distribution:** Tailoring promotional and distribution strategies to the PLC stage enhances marketing effectiveness and ensures the product reaches the target audience at the right time.

Product Life Cycle Extension: Extending the PLC involves strategies to prolong the maturity stage and delay the decline, maximizing the product's profitability and market presence.

Strategies for PLC Extension:

1. **Product Improvements:** Enhance the product with new features, improved quality, or updated designs to attract new customers and retain existing ones.
2. **Market Expansion:** Enter new geographic markets or target new customer segments to increase sales and extend the product's reach.
3. **Rebranding and Repositioning:** Refresh the product's brand image or reposition it in the market to appeal to changing consumer preferences or new trends.
4. **Promotional Activities:** Implement targeted promotional campaigns, special offers, or loyalty programs to boost sales and maintain customer interest.
5. **Product Line Extensions:** Introduce new variants, such as different sizes, flavors, or packaging, to cater to diverse customer needs and preferences.

Product Life Cycle Management (PLM)

Product Life Cycle Management (PLM) is a systematic approach to managing a product's entire lifecycle, from concept and design to production, marketing, and eventual disposal. PLM integrates people, processes, and technology to optimize product development and management.

Key Components of PLM:

1. **Concept and Design:**

   - **Innovation:** Generate and evaluate new product ideas based on market research and customer insights.
   - **Design and Engineering:** Develop detailed designs, prototypes, and specifications, ensuring the product meets quality and performance standards.

2. **Development and Production:**

   - **Collaboration:** Foster cross-functional collaboration among R&D, engineering, manufacturing, and marketing teams to streamline product development.
   - **Quality Control:** Implement rigorous quality control processes to ensure consistency and reliability in production.

3. **Marketing and Sales:**

   - **Market Research:** Continuously monitor market trends, customer feedback, and competitive dynamics to inform marketing strategies.
   - **Sales and Distribution:** Develop effective sales and distribution channels to maximize market reach and customer access.

4. **Support and Maintenance:**

   - **Customer Support:** Provide excellent customer service and support to enhance customer satisfaction and loyalty.
   - **Product Updates:** Regularly update and improve the product based on customer feedback and technological advancements.

5. **End-of-Life Management:**

   - **Sustainability:** Implement environmentally friendly practices for product disposal or recycling, minimizing the environmental impact.

- **Discontinuation:** Plan and execute the product phase-out process, ensuring a smooth transition for customers and stakeholders.

Benefits of PLM:

1. **Improved Efficiency:** Streamlines product development and management processes, reducing time-to-market and costs.
2. **Enhanced Collaboration:** Facilitates collaboration across departments and with external partners, improving communication and decision-making.
3. **Quality and Compliance:** Ensures consistent product quality and compliance with regulatory standards, reducing the risk of recalls and penalties.
4. **Innovation:** Encourages continuous innovation and improvement, keeping the product relevant and competitive in the market.
5. **Customer Satisfaction:** Enhances customer satisfaction by delivering high-quality products that meet evolving needs and preferences.

Conclusion

Understanding the Product Life Cycle and effectively managing it through Product Life Cycle Management are essential for a product's success and longevity in the market. By implementing appropriate strategies for each stage of the PLC and leveraging PLM, companies can optimize their product offerings, drive growth, and achieve sustainable business success.

CHAPTER NINETEEN

PRODUCT DIVERSIFICATION

Product Diversification: Objectives and Modification

Product Diversification is a strategic approach where a company expands its product range by adding new products or services. This strategy helps businesses to spread risk, reach new markets, and drive growth. Diversification can be related (expanding into similar product lines) or unrelated (venturing into completely different markets).

Objectives of Product Diversification

1. **Risk Reduction:**

   - **Objective:** Diversifying the product portfolio reduces dependency on a single product or market, thereby spreading risk.
   - **Benefit:** Protects the company from market fluctuations, economic downturns, and changes in consumer preferences.

2. **Revenue Growth:**

   - **Objective:** Introducing new products or services can create additional revenue streams.
   - **Benefit:** Increases overall sales and profitability by tapping into new customer segments and markets.

3. **Market Expansion:**

- ◦ **Objective:** Diversification allows companies to enter new geographic regions or target new customer demographics.
- ◦ **Benefit:** Expands the company's market reach and potential customer base.

4. **Competitive Advantage:**

- ◦ **Objective:** Offering a broader range of products can differentiate a company from its competitors.
- ◦ **Benefit:** Enhances the company's market position and brand strength.

5. **Innovation and Growth:**

- ◦ **Objective:** Encourages innovation by exploring new product ideas and technologies.
- ◦ **Benefit:** Drives continuous improvement and keeps the company relevant in a rapidly changing market.

6. **Resource Optimization:**

- ◦ **Objective:** Utilizes existing resources, such as technology, expertise, and distribution channels, more effectively.
- ◦ **Benefit:** Maximizes the return on investment and improves operational efficiency.

Product Modification

Product Modification involves making changes to existing products to improve their features, performance, or appeal. This can help in extending the product lifecycle, meeting changing customer needs, and staying competitive.

Types of Product Modification:

1. **Quality Modification:**

- ◦ **Description:** Improving the quality of a product to enhance its performance, durability, or reliability.

- **Example:** Upgrading the materials used in a smartphone to increase its durability.

2. **Feature Modification:**

   - **Description:** Adding new features or enhancing existing ones to make the product more attractive or useful.
   - **Example:** Introducing new software features in a smartwatch.

3. **Style Modification:**

   - **Description:** Changing the product's design, packaging, or appearance to make it more appealing.
   - **Example:** Redesigning the packaging of a beverage to make it more eye-catching.

4. **Functional Modification:**

   - **Description:** Improving the product's functionality or usability.
   - **Example:** Adding a new safety feature to a car model.

Benefits of Product Modification

1. **Customer Satisfaction:**

   - **Benefit:** Meets changing customer preferences and expectations, leading to higher satisfaction and loyalty.

2. **Competitive Edge:**

   - **Benefit:** Keeps the product relevant and competitive in the market by offering improved or unique features.

3. **Extended Product Life Cycle:**

   - **Benefit:** Extends the life of a product by keeping it up-to-date and appealing to consumers.

4. **Market Adaptation:**

   - **Benefit:** Adapts the product to new market trends, technological advancements, and regulatory requirements.

5. **Brand Perception:**

   - **Benefit:** Enhances the brand's image and perception by continuously delivering high-quality and innovative products.

Conclusion

Product diversification and modification are essential strategies for companies to stay competitive, grow, and meet evolving customer needs. By diversifying their product offerings and continuously improving existing products, businesses can achieve long-term success and sustainability.

CHAPTER TWENTY

PRICING STRATEGY

Pricing Strategy: A Comprehensive Guide
Pricing Mix and Definition
Definition: A Pricing Strategy is a method used by businesses to determine the price of their products or services. This strategy considers factors such as costs, competition, target market, and company objectives to set a price that maximizes profitability and market share.

Pricing Mix: The pricing mix, part of the marketing mix (4 Ps: Product, Price, Place, Promotion), involves various elements that influence pricing decisions, such as the cost of production, distribution channels, and competitive landscape.

Importance and Objectives of Pricing
Importance:

1. **Revenue Generation:** Pricing directly affects revenue and profitability. Correct pricing ensures that the business can cover costs and generate a profit.
2. **Market Positioning:** Pricing helps position the product in the market, conveying its perceived value and quality.
3. **Customer Perception:** Pricing influences customer perception of the product's value and can attract or repel certain customer segments.
4. **Competitive Advantage:** Strategic pricing can provide a competitive edge in the market.

Objectives:

1. **Profit Maximization:** Setting prices to achieve the highest possible profit margins.

2. **Market Penetration:** Using lower prices to enter and capture a larger market share.
3. **Survival:** Pricing to cover costs and stay in business during tough economic times.
4. **Market Skimming:** Setting high prices initially and lowering them over time to maximize revenue from different customer segments.
5. **Product Quality Leadership:** Pricing to reflect high quality and establish the product as a premium offering.
6. **Customer Satisfaction:** Setting prices that deliver value to customers and meet their expectations.

Factors Influencing Pricing Decision

1. **Costs:** The total cost of producing, distributing, and selling the product, including fixed and variable costs.
2. **Demand:** The relationship between price and the quantity demanded by customers. Understanding price elasticity of demand is crucial.
3. **Competition:** Competitors' pricing strategies and the level of competition in the market influence pricing decisions.
4. **Market Conditions:** Economic conditions, market trends, and consumer purchasing power.
5. **Company Objectives:** The business's overall goals, such as profitability, market share, or growth.
6. **Customer Perceptions:** How customers perceive the value and quality of the product.
7. **Regulatory Environment:** Legal and regulatory constraints on pricing, such as price controls or anti-trust laws.
8. **Product Lifecycle:** The stage of the product in its life cycle (introduction, growth, maturity, decline).

Process of Price Determination

1. **Market Research:** Conduct thorough research to understand market conditions, customer preferences, and competitive landscape.
2. **Cost Analysis:** Calculate the total cost of producing and delivering the product, including fixed and variable costs.
3. **Demand Analysis:** Assess the demand for the product and determine its price elasticity.

4. **Pricing Objectives:** Define the business's pricing objectives, such as profit maximization, market penetration, or competitive positioning.
5. **Competitive Analysis:** Evaluate competitors' pricing strategies and market position.
6. **Pricing Strategy Selection:** Choose an appropriate pricing strategy based on the gathered data and analysis.
7. **Price Setting:** Set the initial price for the product based on the selected strategy.
8. **Price Testing:** Test the price in the market through limited launches or focus groups to gather feedback.
9. **Price Adjustment:** Adjust the price based on feedback, market response, and ongoing analysis.
10. **Continuous Monitoring:** Regularly monitor the market, costs, and competitive landscape to make necessary pricing adjustments.

Kinds of Pricing and Pricing Methods

1. **Cost-Based Pricing:**

   - **Cost-Plus Pricing:** Adding a standard markup to the cost of the product.
   - **Break-Even Pricing:** Setting the price to cover costs and achieve a break-even point.

2. **Value-Based Pricing:**

   - **Perceived Value Pricing:** Setting the price based on customers' perceived value of the product.
   - **Performance-Based Pricing:** Pricing based on the performance and benefits delivered by the product.

3. **Competition-Based Pricing:**

   - **Going-Rate Pricing:** Setting the price based on competitors' prices.
   - **Price Matching:** Matching competitors' prices to remain competitive in the market.

4. **Demand-Based Pricing:**

- **Dynamic Pricing:** Adjusting prices based on real-time demand and supply conditions.
- **Price Skimming:** Setting high prices initially and lowering them over time.
- **Penetration Pricing:** Setting low prices initially to gain market share quickly.

5. **Psychological Pricing:**

- **Charm Pricing:** Setting prices slightly below a round number (e.g., $9.99 instead of $10.00).
- **Prestige Pricing:** Setting higher prices to convey premium quality and exclusivity.

6. **Bundle Pricing:**

- Offering multiple products together at a reduced price compared to purchasing each separately.

7. **Geographical Pricing:**

- Adjusting prices based on geographic location, considering factors such as shipping costs and regional market conditions.

8. **Freemium Pricing:**

- Offering a basic version of the product for free while charging for premium features or services.

Conclusion

A well-defined pricing strategy is essential for achieving business objectives, maintaining competitiveness, and delivering value to customers. By understanding the various factors influencing pricing decisions and choosing the right pricing methods, companies can optimize their pricing strategies to maximize profitability and market success.

CHAPTER TWENTY-ONE

INTRODUCTION TO DISTRIBUTION

Distribution refers to the process of delivering a product or service from the manufacturer or producer to the end consumer. It encompasses all activities involved in the transfer of goods, including transportation, warehousing, inventory management, and the selection of distribution channels. Effective distribution ensures that products are available to consumers in the right place, at the right time, and in the right quantity.

Functions of Distribution

1. **Transportation:** Moving products from the place of production to various points of sale or storage. Efficient transportation ensures timely delivery and reduces costs.
2. **Warehousing:** Storing products until they are needed for sale. Warehouses protect goods from damage and ensure a steady supply to meet demand.
3. **Inventory Management:** Maintaining optimal inventory levels to meet customer demand without overstocking. Effective inventory management reduces holding costs and minimizes stockouts.
4. **Order Processing:** Handling customer orders efficiently and accurately. This includes receiving orders, processing payments, and preparing shipments.
5. **Market Coverage:** Ensuring products are available in various geographic locations and market segments to maximize reach and sales.
6. **Packaging and Labeling:** Protecting products during transportation and providing necessary information to consumers. Packaging also enhances product appeal.

7. **Customer Service:** Providing support and assistance to customers throughout the distribution process. This includes handling inquiries, complaints, and returns.
8. **Retailing:** Selling products directly to consumers through various retail formats, such as physical stores, online platforms, and catalogs.

Types of Distribution

1. **Direct Distribution:** The manufacturer or producer sells products directly to the end consumer without intermediaries. This can be done through company-owned stores, websites, or direct sales teams.

   - **Example:** Apple selling its products through Apple Stores and its website.

2. **Indirect Distribution:** Involves intermediaries such as wholesalers, distributors, and retailers who help move the product from the manufacturer to the consumer.

   - **Example:** A food manufacturer using wholesalers and retailers to distribute products to grocery stores.

3. **Intensive Distribution:** A strategy where products are stocked in as many outlets as possible to maximize exposure and sales. Commonly used for convenience products.

   - **Example:** Soft drinks and snack foods available in supermarkets, convenience stores, and vending machines.

4. **Selective Distribution:** The manufacturer selects a limited number of intermediaries to carry its products. This approach balances market coverage and control over the distribution process. Often used for shopping products.

   - **Example:** Electronics brands distributing through select retailers and specialty stores.

5. **Exclusive Distribution:** The manufacturer grants exclusive rights to a single distributor or retailer in a specific geographic area. This strategy is used for high-end or luxury products that require a more controlled environment.

    ◦ **Example:** Luxury car brands partnering with exclusive dealerships.

Significance of Channel Decisions

Channel decisions play a crucial role in a company's overall marketing strategy and can significantly impact its success. Here's why they are important:

1. **Market Reach:** Selecting the right distribution channels ensures that products reach the target market effectively, maximizing sales and market penetration.
2. **Cost Efficiency:** Efficient channel management can reduce distribution costs, including transportation, warehousing, and inventory management, leading to better profit margins.
3. **Customer Convenience:** Providing multiple and convenient access points for consumers to purchase products enhances customer satisfaction and loyalty.
4. **Competitive Advantage:** Strategic channel decisions can differentiate a company from its competitors, offering unique value propositions to customers.
5. **Control and Flexibility:** The choice of distribution channels affects the level of control a company has over its product's availability, pricing, and brand image.
6. **Market Feedback:** Effective channels provide valuable feedback from customers and intermediaries, helping companies make informed decisions and improve their offerings.

Factors Determining Choice of Channels
Several factors influence the choice of distribution channels:

1. **Product Characteristics:**

    ◦ **Nature of the Product:** Perishable, fragile, bulky, or complex products may require specific handling and storage conditions, influencing channel selection.

- ◦ **Product Value:** High-value products often use selective or exclusive distribution channels to maintain brand image and ensure proper handling.

2. **Market Characteristics:**

- ◦ **Customer Preferences:** Understanding where and how customers prefer to purchase products helps in selecting appropriate channels.
- ◦ **Geographic Coverage:** The need to reach customers in different geographic locations affects channel choices.

3. **Company Objectives and Resources:**

- ◦ **Marketing Goals:** Objectives such as market penetration, brand positioning, and customer service influence channel decisions.
- ◦ **Financial Resources:** The company's budget for distribution, including transportation and inventory costs, impacts channel selection.

4. **Competitive Landscape:**

- ◦ **Competitor Strategies:** Analyzing competitors' distribution channels can provide insights and opportunities for differentiation.
- ◦ **Market Share:** The presence of established competitors in specific channels may influence the choice of alternative or complementary channels.

5. **Intermediary Characteristics:**

- ◦ **Expertise and Reliability:** The capabilities and reliability of intermediaries, such as distributors and retailers, affect channel performance.
- ◦ **Relationships:** Strong relationships with intermediaries can enhance collaboration and ensure better support for the product.

6. **Legal and Regulatory Environment:**

- ○ **Compliance:** Adhering to legal and regulatory requirements, such as trade restrictions and consumer protection laws, influences channel decisions.
- ○ **Ethical Considerations:** Ensuring ethical practices and maintaining a positive brand image through responsible channel choices.

Conclusion

Distribution is a critical component of the marketing mix, influencing how products reach consumers and ultimately determining a company's success in the market. By carefully considering the functions, types, significance, and factors influencing channel decisions, businesses can develop effective distribution strategies that enhance customer satisfaction, drive sales, and achieve organizational goals.

CHAPTER TWENTY-TWO

MIDDLEMEN IN DISTRIBUTION

Definition, Choice, and Functions

Definition: Middlemen, also known as intermediaries, are entities or individuals who act as a link between the producers of goods and the final consumers. They facilitate the distribution process by performing various functions that make it easier for products to reach the end market.

Choice: The selection of middlemen depends on various factors, such as the nature of the product, market characteristics, distribution strategy, and the company's objectives. Businesses carefully evaluate potential intermediaries based on their expertise, reach, reliability, and cost-effectiveness.

Functions of Middlemen:

1. **Transportation:** Middlemen often handle the logistics of moving products from manufacturers to retailers or directly to consumers.
2. **Warehousing:** They provide storage facilities to hold inventory until it is needed by retailers or consumers.
3. **Financing:** Middlemen may offer credit to retailers or even finance their own purchases from manufacturers, helping to ease cash flow issues for both parties.
4. **Risk-Bearing:** They take on the risks associated with the storage and transportation of goods, such as damage, theft, or obsolescence.
5. **Market Information:** Middlemen gather and provide valuable market information to both producers and consumers, helping in decision-making and strategy formulation.

6. **Promotion and Sales:** They engage in promotional activities and sales efforts to increase product visibility and demand.
7. **Assortment and Allocation:** Middlemen often break bulk quantities from manufacturers into smaller, more manageable sizes for retailers or consumers. They also help in sorting and grading products based on quality.

Types of Middlemen

1. **Wholesalers:**

   - **Definition:** Wholesalers buy large quantities of goods from manufacturers and sell them in smaller quantities to retailers, other businesses, or institutional users.
   - **Functions:** Bulk breaking, warehousing, transportation, financing, risk-bearing, and market information.

2. **Retailers:**

   - **Definition:** Retailers sell products directly to the end consumers. They are the final link in the distribution chain.
   - **Functions:** Assortment, stocking, promotion, sales, and customer service.

3. **Distributors:**

   - **Definition:** Distributors are intermediaries who have an exclusive relationship with a manufacturer to sell their products to retailers or other businesses.
   - **Functions:** Warehousing, transportation, order processing, and market coverage.

4. **Agents and Brokers:**

   - **Definition:** Agents and brokers facilitate the sale of goods between producers and buyers without taking ownership of the products. They earn commissions based on sales.
   - **Functions:** Negotiation, market information, and sales promotion.

5. **Dealers:**

  - **Definition:** Dealers are similar to retailers but often specialize in specific product categories, such as automobiles, electronics, or industrial equipment.
  - **Functions:** Sales, customer service, financing options, and after-sales support.

Arguments For and Against Middlemen
For Middlemen:

1. **Efficiency and Expertise:**

  - Middlemen bring expertise and efficiency to the distribution process, ensuring products reach the market quickly and cost-effectively.
  - They have established relationships and networks, which can expedite market entry and penetration.

2. **Market Coverage:**

  - They provide extensive market coverage, reaching consumers in different geographic regions and market segments.
  - Middlemen enable manufacturers to focus on production while they handle distribution and sales.

3. **Risk Mitigation:**

  - By taking on risks such as inventory holding and transportation, middlemen reduce the burden on manufacturers and retailers.
  - They also provide financial support through credit and financing options.

4. **Customer Convenience:**

  - Middlemen make products readily available to consumers through various retail outlets and distribution channels.
  - They offer additional services such as customer support, after-sales service, and product demonstrations.

Against Middlemen:

1. **Increased Costs:**

   - Each intermediary in the distribution chain adds a margin to the product price, increasing the final cost to consumers.
   - Manufacturers may face reduced profit margins due to middlemen's commissions and fees.

2. **Reduced Control:**

   - Relying on middlemen can result in reduced control over the distribution process, pricing, and brand representation.
   - Manufacturers may struggle to maintain consistent product quality and service standards.

3. **Information Asymmetry:**

   - Middlemen may not always share accurate or complete market information with manufacturers, leading to suboptimal decisions.
   - They might prioritize products based on their own interests rather than the manufacturer's goals.

4. **Channel Conflict:**

   - The presence of multiple intermediaries can lead to conflicts of interest and competition within the distribution channel.
   - Misalignment between manufacturers and middlemen regarding marketing and sales strategies can hinder overall performance.

Conclusion

Middlemen play a crucial role in the distribution process by providing essential functions that facilitate the movement of products from manufacturers to consumers. While they offer significant benefits such as market coverage, efficiency, and risk mitigation, they also present challenges such as increased costs and reduced control. Businesses must carefully evaluate their distribution strategies and the role of middlemen to optimize their supply chain and achieve their marketing objectives.

CHAPTER TWENTY-THREE

CHANNEL CONFLICT

Channel Conflict: Types, Causes, and Management

Channel conflict occurs when there is a disagreement or competition between different members of a distribution channel, such as manufacturers, wholesalers, distributors, and retailers. This conflict can disrupt the smooth flow of products and negatively impact sales, customer satisfaction, and overall business performance.

Types of Channel Conflict

1. **Horizontal Conflict:**

   - **Definition:** Occurs between intermediaries at the same level in the distribution channel. For example, two retailers or two distributors may have conflicts.
   - **Example:** Two retailers of the same brand competing for customers in the same geographic area.

2. **Vertical Conflict:**

   - **Definition:** Occurs between different levels of the same distribution channel. For example, conflicts between manufacturers and wholesalers or wholesalers and retailers.
   - **Example:** A manufacturer bypassing a wholesaler to sell directly to retailers, causing tension with the wholesaler.

3. **Multi-Channel Conflict:**

- **Definition**: Arises when a manufacturer uses multiple distribution channels to reach the same market, leading to conflicts among those channels.
- **Example**: A company selling its products both online and through traditional retail stores, causing conflicts over pricing and customer acquisition.

Causes of Channel Conflict

1. **Incompatible Goals:**

   - Different channel members may have conflicting objectives, such as maximizing profit margins or increasing market share, leading to disagreements.

2. **Pricing Discrepancies:**

   - Variations in pricing strategies among channel members can lead to conflicts. For example, a retailer selling products at a discount while other retailers maintain higher prices.

3. **Territorial Issues:**

   - Overlapping territories or market areas can cause conflicts among channel members competing for the same customers.

4. **Resource Allocation:**

   - Competition for limited resources, such as promotional support or inventory, can lead to conflicts among channel members.

5. **Communication Breakdown:**

   - Lack of clear and effective communication among channel members can result in misunderstandings and conflicts.

6. **Product Allocation:**

- Disputes may arise when certain channel members receive preferential treatment in terms of product availability or exclusive deals.

7. **Changes in Distribution Strategy:**

   - Introducing new distribution channels or altering existing ones can create conflicts with current channel members.

Management of Channel Conflict

1. **Clear Communication:**

   - Establish open and transparent communication channels to ensure that all members are aware of each other's roles, responsibilities, and goals. Regular meetings and updates can help prevent misunderstandings.

2. **Conflict Resolution Mechanisms:**

   - Implement formal conflict resolution mechanisms, such as mediation or arbitration, to address disputes in a structured manner.

3. **Channel Policies:**

   - Develop and enforce clear channel policies that outline guidelines for pricing, territory allocation, and resource distribution. Ensure that all channel members adhere to these policies.

4. **Training and Support:**

   - Provide training and support to channel members to align their goals with the overall objectives of the distribution network. This can include sales training, marketing support, and customer service initiatives.

5. **Incentive Programs:**

- Create incentive programs that reward collaboration and performance. Offer bonuses, discounts, or other incentives to channel members who achieve sales targets and work cooperatively.

6. **Market Segmentation:**

    - Segment the market and allocate specific territories or customer segments to different channel members to reduce direct competition.

7. **Dual Distribution Management:**

    - When using multiple distribution channels, ensure that each channel has a distinct role and target market to minimize overlap and conflicts. Develop strategies to manage and coordinate multi-channel efforts effectively.

8. **Feedback Mechanisms:**

    - Implement feedback mechanisms to gather input from channel members regularly. Use this feedback to identify potential issues and make necessary adjustments to the distribution strategy.

9. **Relationship Building:**

    - Invest in building strong relationships with channel members based on trust, mutual respect, and collaboration. Foster a sense of partnership to work towards common goals.

Conclusion

Channel conflict is a common challenge in distribution networks, but with proactive management and clear communication, it can be minimized or resolved. By understanding the types and causes of channel conflict and implementing effective management strategies, businesses can maintain a harmonious and efficient distribution system that drives sales and customer satisfaction.

CHAPTER TWENTY-FOUR

WHOLESALERS

Channel Conflict: Types, Causes, and Management

Channel conflict occurs when there is a disagreement or competition between different members of a distribution channel, such as manufacturers, wholesalers, distributors, and retailers. This conflict can disrupt the smooth flow of products and negatively impact sales, customer satisfaction, and overall business performance.

Types of Channel Conflict

1. **Horizontal Conflict:**

    - **Definition:** Occurs between intermediaries at the same level in the distribution channel. For example, two retailers or two distributors may have conflicts.
    - **Example:** Two retailers of the same brand competing for customers in the same geographic area.

2. **Vertical Conflict:**

    - **Definition:** Occurs between different levels of the same distribution channel. For example, conflicts between manufacturers and wholesalers or wholesalers and retailers.
    - **Example:** A manufacturer bypassing a wholesaler to sell directly to retailers, causing tension with the wholesaler.

3. **Multi-Channel Conflict:**

- **Definition:** Arises when a manufacturer uses multiple distribution channels to reach the same market, leading to conflicts among those channels.
- **Example:** A company selling its products both online and through traditional retail stores, causing conflicts over pricing and customer acquisition.

Causes of Channel Conflict

1. **Incompatible Goals:**

   - Different channel members may have conflicting objectives, such as maximizing profit margins or increasing market share, leading to disagreements.

2. **Pricing Discrepancies:**

   - Variations in pricing strategies among channel members can lead to conflicts. For example, a retailer selling products at a discount while other retailers maintain higher prices.

3. **Territorial Issues:**

   - Overlapping territories or market areas can cause conflicts among channel members competing for the same customers.

4. **Resource Allocation:**

   - Competition for limited resources, such as promotional support or inventory, can lead to conflicts among channel members.

5. **Communication Breakdown:**

   - Lack of clear and effective communication among channel members can result in misunderstandings and conflicts.

6. **Product Allocation:**

- Disputes may arise when certain channel members receive preferential treatment in terms of product availability or exclusive deals.

7. **Changes in Distribution Strategy:**

- Introducing new distribution channels or altering existing ones can create conflicts with current channel members.

Management of Channel Conflict

1. **Clear Communication:**

- Establish open and transparent communication channels to ensure that all members are aware of each other's roles, responsibilities, and goals. Regular meetings and updates can help prevent misunderstandings.

2. **Conflict Resolution Mechanisms:**

- Implement formal conflict resolution mechanisms, such as mediation or arbitration, to address disputes in a structured manner.

3. **Channel Policies:**

- Develop and enforce clear channel policies that outline guidelines for pricing, territory allocation, and resource distribution. Ensure that all channel members adhere to these policies.

4. **Training and Support:**

- Provide training and support to channel members to align their goals with the overall objectives of the distribution network. This can include sales training, marketing support, and customer service initiatives.

5. **Incentive Programs:**

- Create incentive programs that reward collaboration and performance. Offer bonuses, discounts, or other incentives to channel members who achieve sales targets and work cooperatively.

6. **Market Segmentation:**

   - Segment the market and allocate specific territories or customer segments to different channel members to reduce direct competition.

7. **Dual Distribution Management:**

   - When using multiple distribution channels, ensure that each channel has a distinct role and target market to minimize overlap and conflicts. Develop strategies to manage and coordinate multi-channel efforts effectively.

8. **Feedback Mechanisms:**

   - Implement feedback mechanisms to gather input from channel members regularly. Use this feedback to identify potential issues and make necessary adjustments to the distribution strategy.

9. **Relationship Building:**

   - Invest in building strong relationships with channel members based on trust, mutual respect, and collaboration. Foster a sense of partnership to work towards common goals.

Conclusion

Channel conflict is a common challenge in distribution networks, but with proactive management and clear communication, it can be minimized or resolved. By understanding the types and causes of channel conflict and implementing effective management strategies, businesses can maintain a harmonious and efficient distribution system that drives sales and customer satisfaction.

CHAPTER TWENTY-FIVE

RETAILERS

Retailers are businesses or individuals that sell goods and services directly to the end consumers for personal or household use. They act as intermediaries in the distribution channel, providing the final link between manufacturers or wholesalers and the ultimate buyers. Retailers offer a variety of products, facilitate convenient access for consumers, and often provide additional services such as customer support and product demonstrations.

Characteristics, Functions, and Types
Characteristics of Retailers:

1. **Consumer-Centric:** Retailers are focused on meeting the needs and preferences of the end consumers.
2. **Assortment:** They offer a wide range of products, providing consumers with multiple choices and options.
3. **Convenience:** Retailers make products easily accessible to consumers, both in terms of location and availability.
4. **Service-Oriented:** They often provide additional services such as customer support, product demonstrations, and after-sales services.
5. **Promotion:** Retailers engage in promotional activities to attract customers and drive sales.

Functions of Retailers:

1. **Breaking Bulk:** Retailers purchase large quantities from wholesalers or manufacturers and sell them in smaller, more manageable quantities to consumers.

2. **Providing Assortment:** They offer a variety of products from different brands and categories, giving consumers the convenience of one-stop shopping.
3. **Holding Inventory:** Retailers stock products to ensure they are readily available to consumers, reducing the need for consumers to store large quantities at home.
4. **Providing Information:** Retailers gather and disseminate information about products, prices, and availability to consumers.
5. **Facilitating Transactions:** They handle the sales process, including processing payments, managing returns, and offering credit options.

Types of Retailers:

1. **Department Stores:** Large retail establishments offering a wide range of products, organized into various departments (e.g., clothing, electronics, home goods).
2. **Specialty Stores:** Retailers that focus on a specific category of products, such as electronics, books, or sporting goods.
3. **Supermarkets:** Large stores that primarily sell food and grocery items, often with additional sections for household goods.
4. **Convenience Stores:** Small stores located in residential areas, offering a limited range of everyday items such as snacks, beverages, and basic groceries.
5. **Discount Stores:** Retailers that offer products at lower prices by minimizing overhead costs (e.g., Dollar Stores, Big Bazaar).
6. **Online Retailers:** E-commerce platforms that sell products through websites and mobile apps (e.g., Amazon, Flipkart).
7. **Warehouse Clubs:** Membership-based stores that sell products in bulk at discounted prices (e.g., Costco).

Services Provided by Retailers

1. **Product Information:** Retailers provide detailed information about products, including features, usage instructions, and benefits, helping consumers make informed decisions.
2. **Customer Support:** Offering assistance with product selection, answering queries, and providing after-sales services such as returns and exchanges.

3. **Home Delivery:** Many retailers offer delivery services, bringing products directly to consumers' homes.
4. **Financing Options:** Providing credit, installment plans, and layaway options to make purchases more affordable.
5. **Product Demonstrations:** Offering demonstrations or samples to help consumers experience products before purchasing.
6. **Loyalty Programs:** Retailers often have loyalty programs that reward customers with discounts, points, or exclusive offers for repeat purchases.
7. **Gift Wrapping:** Providing gift-wrapping services for special occasions.

Advantages and Disadvantages of Small and Large-Scale Retail Businesses
Small-Scale Retail Businesses:
Advantages:

1. **Personalized Service:** Small retailers can offer more personalized and attentive customer service.
2. **Flexibility:** They can quickly adapt to changes in consumer preferences and market trends.
3. **Community Focus:** Small retailers often build strong relationships with local communities and customers.

Disadvantages:

1. **Limited Resources:** Smaller retailers may have fewer financial and operational resources.
2. **Higher Costs:** They may face higher per-unit costs due to lower purchasing volumes and limited economies of scale.
3. **Limited Market Reach:** Small retailers may have a limited geographic reach and customer base.

Large-Scale Retail Businesses:
Advantages:

1. **Economies of Scale:** Large retailers benefit from lower per-unit costs due to bulk purchasing and efficient operations.

2. **Wide Assortment:** They can offer a vast range of products, providing customers with more choices.
3. **Market Presence:** Large retailers often have a strong market presence and extensive geographic reach.

Disadvantages:

1. **Impersonal Service:** Large retailers may struggle to provide personalized customer service.
2. **Inflexibility:** They may be slower to adapt to changes in consumer preferences and market conditions.
3. **Operational Complexity:** Managing large-scale operations can be complex and challenging.

Types of Retail Institutions

1. **Chain Stores:** Multiple retail outlets under common ownership and standardized management, offering consistency across locations (e.g., Walmart, Starbucks).
2. **Independent Retailers:** Single-store operations owned and managed by individuals or small groups, offering unique and personalized shopping experiences.
3. **Franchises:** Retail outlets operated by franchisees under the brand and business model of a franchisor (e.g., McDonald's, Subway).
4. **Cooperatives:** Retailers owned and operated by a group of members who share in the profits and decision-making (e.g., cooperative grocery stores).
5. **Superstores and Hypermarkets:** Very large retail stores offering a wide range of products, including groceries, electronics, clothing, and household goods (e.g., Carrefour, Tesco).
6. **Category Killers:** Large specialty stores that dominate a specific product category, often driving out smaller competitors (e.g., Best Buy, Home Depot).

Conclusion

Retailers play a vital role in the distribution process by making products accessible to consumers and providing valuable services. Understanding the characteristics, functions, and types of retailers, as well as the advantages and disadvantages of different retail scales, helps businesses develop effective retail strategies that enhance customer satisfaction and drive sales.

CHAPTER TWENTY-SIX

SALES PROMOTION

Meaning and Definition: Sales Promotion refers to a variety of marketing techniques aimed at boosting the sales of a product or service in the short term. These techniques are designed to stimulate consumer demand, increase product visibility, and drive immediate sales.

Objectives:

1. **Increase Sales:** Drive immediate sales by offering incentives that encourage consumers to make a purchase.
2. **Attract New Customers:** Entice new customers to try the product or service through special offers or discounts.
3. **Retain Existing Customers:** Reward loyal customers with exclusive deals and promotions to foster long-term relationships.
4. **Introduce New Products:** Generate excitement and interest around new product launches.
5. **Clear Inventory:** Move excess or outdated inventory to free up space for new products.
6. **Enhance Brand Awareness:** Increase brand visibility and recognition through promotional activities.

Importance and Marketing Communication Process
Importance:
Boosts Sales: Sales promotions can lead to a significant increase in sales volume and revenue.

Encourages Trial: Promotions encourage consumers to try new products, leading to potential long-term adoption.

Builds Customer Loyalty: Rewarding loyal customers with promotions fosters a strong relationship and encourages repeat purchases.

Competitive Advantage: Effective sales promotions can give a company a competitive edge in the market.

Market Penetration: Helps in penetrating new markets and expanding the customer base.

Marketing Communication Process:

1. **Sender:** The company or brand initiating the promotion.
2. **Encoding:** Translating the promotional message into a format that can be communicated, such as an advertisement or coupon.
3. **Message:** The actual content of the promotion, including the offer and call to action.
4. **Medium:** The channels used to deliver the message, such as TV, radio, social media, or in-store displays.
5. **Receiver:** The target audience or consumers who receive the promotional message.
6. **Decoding:** The process by which the target audience interprets and understands the promotional message.
7. **Feedback:** The response from the target audience, such as increased sales, inquiries, or engagement.
8. **Noise:** Any external factors that can distort or interfere with the message delivery, such as competing promotions or poor communication.

Promotional Methods, Planning Stages, and Strategies
Promotional Methods:

1. **Discounts and Coupons:** Offering price reductions or coupons to incentivize purchases.
2. **Contests and Sweepstakes:** Engaging consumers through competitions and prize draws.
3. **Samples and Trial Offers:** Providing free samples or trial periods to encourage product trials.
4. **Rebates and Cashbacks:** Offering money back after purchase as an incentive.
5. **Loyalty Programs:** Rewarding repeat customers with points or discounts.
6. **Point-of-Purchase Displays:** Attractive in-store displays to catch consumers' attention.
7. **Bundling:** Selling products together at a reduced price.

Planning Stages:

1. **Objective Setting:** Define the goals and objectives of the promotion.
2. **Budgeting:** Allocate resources and set a budget for the promotional activities.
3. **Message Development:** Create the promotional message and materials.
4. **Channel Selection:** Choose the appropriate channels for delivering the promotion.
5. **Implementation:** Execute the promotional activities.
6. **Monitoring and Evaluation:** Track the performance of the promotion and assess its effectiveness.

Strategies:

1. **Pull Strategy:** Focus on creating demand among consumers who then request the product from retailers.
2. **Push Strategy:** Encourage retailers and distributors to promote the product to end consumers.
3. **Hybrid Strategy:** Combine both pull and push strategies for maximum impact.

Techniques, Merits, and Demerits
Techniques:

1. **Price Promotions:** Temporary price reductions, discounts, or special offers.
2. **Coupons:** Vouchers that provide a discount on the next purchase.
3. **Sampling:** Distributing free samples to encourage product trials.
4. **Premiums:** Offering free or discounted products as a bonus with purchases.
5. **Loyalty Programs:** Rewarding customers for repeat purchases.

Merits:

1. **Immediate Sales Boost:** Quick increase in sales volume.
2. **Customer Attraction:** Attracts new customers and encourages trials.
3. **Inventory Clearance:** Helps in moving excess stock.
4. **Brand Awareness:** Increases visibility and recognition.

5. **Customer Engagement:** Engages customers and builds loyalty.

Demerits:

1. **Temporary Impact:** Sales promotions often have short-term effects.
2. **Profit Margin Erosion:** Discounts and offers can reduce profit margins.
3. **Customer Expectation:** Frequent promotions may lead customers to expect continuous discounts.
4. **Brand Perception:** Over-reliance on promotions can affect brand perception negatively.
5. **Complexity:** Managing and executing promotions can be complex and resource-intensive.

Types and Importance of Sales Promotions
Types:

1. **Consumer Promotions:** Targeted at end consumers, such as discounts, coupons, samples, and loyalty programs.
2. **Trade Promotions:** Aimed at retailers and distributors, including trade allowances, display allowances, and trade shows.
3. **Sales Force Promotions:** Incentives for the sales team to boost performance, such as bonuses, contests, and recognition programs.

Importance:

- **Drives Short-Term Sales:** Provides a quick boost to sales and revenue.
- **Encourages Product Trials:** Promotes new product adoption by reducing perceived risk.
- **Clears Inventory:** Moves old or excess stock quickly.
- **Enhances Customer Loyalty:** Strengthens relationships with existing customers.
- **Increases Market Penetration:** Helps in reaching new customers and expanding market presence.

Steps in Promotion Decisions

1. **Identify Objectives:** Define the goals of the promotion, such as increasing sales, introducing a new product, or enhancing brand

awareness.

2. **Select Target Audience:** Identify the specific consumer segment to target with the promotion.
3. **Determine Budget:** Allocate financial resources for the promotion based on objectives and expected ROI.
4. **Choose Promotion Type:** Decide on the promotional method, such as discounts, contests, or loyalty programs.
5. **Develop Message:** Create a compelling promotional message that resonates with the target audience.
6. **Select Channels:** Choose the appropriate communication channels to reach the target audience.
7. **Implement Promotion:** Execute the promotional activities according to the plan.
8. **Evaluate Results:** Measure the effectiveness of the promotion against the set objectives and make adjustments if necessary.

Promotional Mix

Promotional Mix refers to the combination of various promotional tools and methods used to achieve marketing objectives. The key components of the promotional mix include:

1. **Advertising:** Paid, non-personal communication through various media channels to promote products and services.
2. **Sales Promotion:** Short-term incentives to encourage immediate purchase or engagement.
3. **Public Relations (PR):** Managing the public image and reputation of the company through media relations, events, and communication strategies.
4. **Personal Selling:** Direct interaction between sales representatives and customers to persuade and close sales.
5. **Direct Marketing:** Communicating directly with customers through mail, email, telemarketing, or digital platforms to generate a response or transaction.
6. **Digital Marketing:** Online marketing efforts, including social media, search engine marketing, content marketing, and email marketing.

Conclusion

Sales promotion is a vital component of the marketing mix that provides short-term incentives to boost sales, attract new customers, and enhance brand awareness. By understanding the various aspects of sales promotion, including its meaning, objectives, importance, methods, and strategies, businesses can effectively plan and execute promotional activities that drive growth and achieve marketing goals.

CHAPTER TWENTY-SEVEN

ADVERTISING

Advertising is a form of communication intended to persuade an audience to purchase products, services, or ideas. It involves paid promotion through various media channels, designed to reach a wide audience and influence their buying behavior.

Features of Advertising

1. **Non-Personal Communication:** Advertising delivers messages to a broad audience without direct interaction.
2. **Paid Promotion:** Advertisers invest money to disseminate their messages through chosen media channels.
3. **Identified Sponsor:** The advertiser's identity is clearly mentioned in the advertisement.
4. **Persuasive Intent:** The main goal is to persuade the audience to take specific actions, such as making a purchase.
5. **Creative Presentation:** Advertisements use creative elements like visuals, slogans, and jingles to engage the audience.
6. **Repetition:** Ads are often repeated to reinforce the message and increase recall.

Main Purposes of Advertising

1. **Informing:** Provide information about products or services to create awareness and educate the target audience.
2. **Persuading:** Convince potential customers to choose a product or service by highlighting its benefits and differentiating it from competitors.

3. **Reminding:** Keep the brand or product top-of-mind for consumers, especially in competitive markets.
4. **Reinforcing:** Strengthen existing customer relationships and brand loyalty by reminding customers of their positive experiences.
5. **Positioning:** Establish a unique position for the brand or product in the minds of consumers.

Advantages and Importance of Advertising
Advantages:

1. **Wide Reach:** Advertising can reach a large and diverse audience through various media channels.
2. **Brand Awareness:** Helps build and maintain brand awareness and recognition.
3. **Market Penetration:** Facilitates market entry and expansion by introducing products to new customers and markets.
4. **Sales Promotion:** Drives sales by persuading customers to purchase products and services.
5. **Competitive Advantage:** Differentiates a brand from its competitors and highlights its unique selling propositions.

Importance:

1. **Economic Growth:** Stimulates demand and consumption, contributing to economic growth and development.
2. **Consumer Education:** Provides valuable information to consumers about new products, features, and benefits, helping them make informed decisions.
3. **Product Launch:** Plays a crucial role in the successful launch of new products and services.
4. **Brand Loyalty:** Fosters brand loyalty and long-term customer relationships through consistent and engaging advertising.
5. **Support for Media:** Advertising revenues support various media outlets, enabling them to provide content and services to the public.

Kinds of Advertising Media

1. **Print Media:**

- ◦ **Newspapers:** Reach a broad audience and provide detailed information.
- ◦ **Magazines:** Target specific interest groups and offer high-quality visuals.

2. **Broadcast Media:**

- ◦ **Television:** Combines audio, visual, and motion elements to create impactful messages.
- ◦ **Radio:** Relies on audio elements and can reach audiences during commutes and other activities.

3. **Digital Media:**

- ◦ **Social Media:** Platforms like Facebook, Instagram, and Twitter allow for targeted advertising and engagement with users.
- ◦ **Search Engines:** Ads appear alongside search results, targeting users based on their search queries.
- ◦ **Websites:** Display ads and banners on websites reach users while they browse online content.

4. **Outdoor Media:**

- ◦ **Billboards:** Large, eye-catching advertisements placed in high-traffic areas.
- ◦ **Transit Advertising:** Ads on buses, trains, taxis, and other forms of public transportation.

5. **Direct Mail:**

- ◦ **Brochures:** Printed materials sent directly to consumers' homes or businesses.
- ◦ **Catalogs:** Comprehensive listings of products and services, often used by retailers.

6. **Public Relations and Events:**

- **Sponsorships:** Brands sponsor events, sports teams, or cultural activities to gain visibility and goodwill.
- **Exhibitions:** Trade shows and exhibitions provide opportunities for direct interaction with potential customers.

7. **Product Placement:**

- **Movies and TV Shows:** Brands are featured within the content of films and television programs, integrating seamlessly with the storyline.

Conclusion

Advertising is a powerful tool that helps businesses communicate with their target audience, build brand awareness, and drive sales. By leveraging various advertising media and employing creative, persuasive techniques, advertisers can achieve their marketing objectives and maintain a competitive edge in the market.

CHAPTER TWENTY-EIGHT

PERSONAL SELLING

Meaning and Concept: Personal Selling is a direct form of communication where sales representatives interact with potential buyers to persuade them to purchase products or services. It involves face-to-face meetings, telephone conversations, or virtual interactions where the salesperson can address individual customer needs and concerns.

Features:

Direct Interaction: Personal selling involves direct, two-way communication between the salesperson and the customer.

Customization: The approach and presentation are tailored to meet the specific needs and preferences of each customer.

Relationship Building: Focuses on building long-term relationships with customers through trust and rapport.

Immediate Feedback: Salespeople can receive instant feedback from customers and adjust their approach accordingly.

Persuasion: The primary goal is to persuade potential customers to make a purchase.

Needs:

Complex Products: Products that require detailed explanation and demonstration benefit from personal selling.

Customization: Products or services that can be customized to meet individual customer needs.

High-Value Transactions: High-cost items where customers need reassurance and personalized attention.

B2B Sales: Business-to-business sales often involve personal selling due to the complexity and high value of transactions.

Basic Characteristics and Benefits

Characteristics:

Interpersonal Skills: Successful personal selling requires strong interpersonal and communication skills.

Product Knowledge: Salespeople must have in-depth knowledge of the products or services they are selling.

Customer Focus: Understanding and addressing customer needs and preferences is crucial.

Adaptability: Salespeople must be flexible and able to adjust their approach based on customer responses.

Persistence: Personal selling often involves overcoming objections and closing deals through persistence.

Benefits:

Customer Satisfaction: Personalized interactions enhance customer satisfaction and loyalty.

Higher Conversion Rates: Direct communication increases the likelihood of closing sales.

Market Insights: Salespeople gather valuable insights into customer preferences and market trends.

Building Relationships: Establishing strong relationships leads to repeat business and referrals.

Product Customization: Salespeople can tailor products or services to meet specific customer needs.

Arguments Against Personal Selling

High Costs: Personal selling can be expensive due to the need for a skilled sales force, travel, and time investment.

Limited Reach: Personal selling typically reaches fewer potential customers compared to mass advertising.

Time-Consuming: Building relationships and closing deals can be time-consuming.

Sales Pressure: Potential customers may feel pressured or uncomfortable with direct selling approaches.

Training Requirements: Salespeople require extensive training and ongoing support to be effective.

Steps and Methods in Personal Selling

Steps in Personal Selling:

Prospecting: Identifying potential customers who may be interested in the product or service.

Pre-Approach: Gathering information about the prospect and planning the sales approach.

Approach: Making initial contact with the prospect, whether in person, by phone, or virtually.

Presentation: Demonstrating the product or service, highlighting its features and benefits.

Handling Objections: Addressing any concerns or objections the prospect may have.

Closing: Persuading the prospect to make a purchase and finalizing the sale.

Follow-Up: Ensuring customer satisfaction and maintaining the relationship for future sales.

Methods in Personal Selling:

Consultative Selling: Acting as an advisor to the customer, focusing on solving their problems.

Needs-Based Selling: Identifying and addressing the specific needs of the customer.

Solution Selling: Providing a comprehensive solution to the customer's challenges.

Relationship Selling: Building long-term relationships with customers based on trust and mutual benefit.

Advantages and Limitations

Advantages:

Customized Approach: Tailored presentations and solutions based on individual customer needs.

Immediate Feedback: Ability to address customer concerns and adjust the approach in real-time.

Relationship Building: Establishing strong, personal relationships with customers.

Higher Closing Rates: Increased likelihood of closing sales through direct interaction.

Limitations:

Costly: High costs associated with hiring, training, and maintaining a sales force.

Limited Reach: Ability to reach a smaller audience compared to mass marketing methods.

Time-Intensive: Requires significant time investment to build relationships and close sales.

Sales Pressure: Potential for customers to feel pressured or uncomfortable with direct selling.

Functions, Duties, and Responsibilities of Salesmen

Functions:

Generating Leads: Identifying and qualifying potential customers.

Presenting Products: Demonstrating and explaining product features and benefits.

Handling Objections: Addressing customer concerns and overcoming objections.

Closing Sales: Persuading customers to make a purchase.

Providing After-Sales Service: Ensuring customer satisfaction and handling any issues post-purchase.

Duties and Responsibilities:

Prospecting: Continuously identifying and qualifying new prospects.

Product Knowledge: Maintaining in-depth knowledge of products and services.

Customer Relations: Building and nurturing relationships with customers.

Sales Reporting: Tracking sales activities and reporting progress to management.

Target Achievement: Meeting or exceeding sales targets and quotas.

Types of Salesmen

Inside Salesmen: Work from the office, handling sales over the phone or through virtual communication.

Outside Salesmen: Travel to meet customers in person, often covering specific territories.

Technical Salesmen: Specialize in selling complex products that require technical knowledge.

Retail Salesmen: Work in retail environments, assisting customers in selecting and purchasing products.

Wholesale Salesmen: Sell products in bulk to retailers or other businesses.

Consultative Salesmen: Act as advisors, providing solutions based on customer needs.

Difference Between Advertising and Personal Selling

Feature	Advertising	Personal Selling
Nature	Mass communication	Direct, interpersonal communication
Interaction	One-way	Two-way
Cost	Lower cost per reach	Higher cost per customer
Reach	Broad audience	Limited, targeted audience
Customization	Standardized message	Customized approach
Feedback	Delayed or indirect	Immediate and direct
Relationship	Limited relationship building	Strong relationship building

CHAPTER TWENTY-NINE

GLOBAL MARKETING

Global Marketing: Importance, Pros, and Cons

Global Marketing refers to the process of planning, producing, placing, and promoting products or services in the worldwide market. It involves tailoring marketing strategies to meet the needs and preferences of consumers in different countries and regions.

Importance of Global Marketing

1. **Market Expansion:** By entering new international markets, companies can significantly increase their customer base and revenue potential.
2. **Economies of Scale:** Global marketing allows companies to achieve economies of scale in production, distribution, and marketing, reducing overall costs.
3. **Brand Recognition:** A global presence enhances brand recognition and credibility, making it easier to attract customers and partners in new markets.
4. **Diversification:** Expanding into multiple markets diversifies revenue streams, reducing dependence on any single market and mitigating risks associated with economic downturns or political instability.
5. **Innovation:** Exposure to diverse markets and consumer preferences fosters innovation and the development of new products and services.
6. **Competitive Advantage:** A well-executed global marketing strategy can provide a competitive edge by positioning the brand as a global leader.

Pros of Global Marketing

1. **Increased Revenue:** Access to new markets and a larger customer base can lead to higher sales and profits.

2. **Growth Opportunities:** Expanding internationally opens up new growth opportunities and market potential.
3. **Enhanced Brand Image:** Being a global brand enhances the company's image and reputation, attracting more customers and partners.
4. **Resource Optimization:** Global marketing allows companies to optimize resources by leveraging strengths and capabilities across different markets.
5. **Adaptability:** Companies that engage in global marketing often become more adaptable and responsive to changing market conditions and consumer preferences.
6. **Innovation and Learning:** Operating in diverse markets encourages innovation and learning, driving continuous improvement and development.

Cons of Global Marketing

1. **Cultural Differences:** Understanding and navigating cultural differences can be challenging and may require significant adaptation of marketing strategies.
2. **Legal and Regulatory Compliance:** Each country has its own set of laws and regulations, making compliance complex and time-consuming.
3. **High Costs:** Entering and operating in new markets can be expensive, with costs associated with market research, localization, distribution, and promotion.
4. **Logistical Challenges:** Managing logistics across different countries, including shipping, customs, and inventory management, can be complex and costly.
5. **Political and Economic Risks:** Companies face risks related to political instability, economic fluctuations, and changes in trade policies in different markets.
6. **Brand Dilution:** If not managed carefully, expanding into too many markets can dilute the brand's identity and weaken its overall positioning.

Conclusion

Global marketing offers significant benefits, including increased revenue, growth opportunities, and enhanced brand image. However, it also presents challenges such as cultural differences, legal compliance, and high costs. By carefully planning and executing a global marketing strategy, companies can successfully navigate these challenges and reap the rewards of a global presence.

CHAPTER THIRTY

TELEMARKETING

Telemarketing is a direct marketing method in which sales representatives contact potential or existing customers over the phone to promote products or services, generate leads, conduct market research, or gather customer feedback. It involves personalized communication and can be used for both outbound (initiated by the company) and inbound (initiated by the customer) interactions.

Types of Telemarketing

1. **Outbound Telemarketing:**

   ◦ **Definition:** Sales representatives make unsolicited calls to potential customers to promote products, set appointments, or gather information.
   ◦ **Example:** Calling a list of prospects to offer a new product or service.

2. **Inbound Telemarketing:**

   ◦ **Definition:** Representatives receive calls from customers who are responding to advertisements, seeking information, or making inquiries.
   ◦ **Example:** Handling customer inquiries and orders from an ad campaign.

3. **Lead Generation:**

   ◦ **Definition:** Identifying and qualifying potential customers for follow-up by the sales team.

- ◦ **Example:** Calling prospects to gauge their interest and collect contact information.

4. **Sales Calls:**

   - ◦ **Definition:** Directly selling products or services over the phone.
   - ◦ **Example:** Representatives explaining product features and benefits to close a sale.

5. **Surveys and Research:**

   - ◦ **Definition:** Conducting surveys or market research to gather data on customer preferences, satisfaction, or market trends.
   - ◦ **Example:** Calling customers to ask for feedback on their recent purchase experience.

6. **Appointment Setting:**

   - ◦ **Definition:** Scheduling appointments for sales representatives to meet with potential customers.
   - ◦ **Example:** Calling prospects to arrange a meeting for a product demonstration.

Advantages of Telemarketing

1. **Direct Interaction:** Provides immediate and personalized communication with customers, allowing for real-time feedback and clarification.
2. **Cost-Effective:** Less expensive than face-to-face sales visits and can reach a large number of potential customers in a short time.
3. **Flexibility:** Telemarketing campaigns can be easily adjusted based on real-time results and feedback.
4. **Measurable Results:** Allows for tracking and measurement of campaign performance through metrics such as call duration, conversion rates, and customer responses.
5. **Lead Generation:** Effective in identifying and qualifying potential leads for follow-up by the sales team.

6. **Customer Relationship**: Helps build and maintain relationships with customers through regular communication and follow-ups.

Disadvantages of Telemarketing

1. **Intrusiveness**: Unsolicited calls can be perceived as intrusive and annoying, potentially damaging the company's reputation.
2. **Regulatory Compliance**: Telemarketing is subject to various laws and regulations, such as the Do Not Call (DNC) registry, which can limit its reach and effectiveness.
3. **Negative Perception**: Telemarketing has a negative reputation due to high-pressure sales tactics and scams, leading to customer distrust.
4. **Limited Reach**: It may not be effective for reaching customers who prefer online communication or those who are difficult to contact by phone.
5. **High Rejection Rates**: Telemarketers often face high rejection rates, requiring resilience and persistence.
6. **Training and Quality Control**: Ensuring that telemarketers are well-trained and maintain high-quality communication can be challenging and resource-intensive.

Conclusion

Telemarketing is a versatile and direct marketing method that offers several advantages, such as direct interaction, cost-effectiveness, and flexibility. However, it also faces challenges, including its intrusiveness, regulatory compliance, and negative perception. By carefully planning and executing telemarketing campaigns, businesses can leverage its benefits while mitigating its drawbacks.

CHAPTER THIRTY-ONE

DIGITAL MARKETING

Digital Marketing refers to the use of digital channels, platforms, and technologies to promote products, services, or brands to a targeted audience. It encompasses a wide range of online marketing activities, including search engine optimization (SEO), content marketing, social media marketing, email marketing, and online advertising.

Benefits of Digital Marketing

1. **Global Reach:**

   - **Benefit:** Digital marketing allows businesses to reach a global audience, breaking geographic barriers and expanding market reach.
   - **Example:** A small business can sell products to customers worldwide through an e-commerce website.

2. **Targeted Advertising:**

   - **Benefit:** Digital marketing enables precise targeting based on demographics, interests, behavior, and location.
   - **Example:** Social media platforms like Facebook and Instagram allow advertisers to target specific audience segments with tailored ads.

3. **Cost-Effectiveness:**

   - **Benefit:** Digital marketing can be more cost-effective than traditional marketing methods, allowing businesses of all sizes to compete.
   - **Example:** Pay-per-click (PPC) advertising allows businesses to set budgets and pay only when users click on their ads.

4. **Measurable Results:**

   - ◦ **Benefit:** Digital marketing provides detailed analytics and metrics, allowing businesses to track and measure the effectiveness of their campaigns.
   - ◦ **Example:** Tools like Google Analytics provide insights into website traffic, user behavior, and conversion rates.

5. **Flexibility and Adaptability:**

   - ◦ **Benefit:** Digital marketing campaigns can be easily adjusted and optimized based on real-time data and feedback.
   - ◦ **Example:** Marketers can test different ad creatives, keywords, and audience segments to improve performance.

6. **Enhanced Engagement:**

   - ◦ **Benefit:** Digital marketing allows for direct interaction and engagement with customers through social media, email, and other online channels.
   - ◦ **Example:** Brands can respond to customer inquiries, comments, and reviews on social media platforms.

7. **Higher Conversion Rates:**

   - ◦ **Benefit:** Digital marketing often leads to higher conversion rates due to personalized and targeted messaging.
   - ◦ **Example:** Email marketing campaigns with personalized content and offers can drive higher open and click-through rates.

Disadvantages of Digital Marketing

1. **Intense Competition:**

   - ◦ **Disadvantage:** The digital landscape is highly competitive, making it challenging for businesses to stand out and capture audience attention.

  - **Example:** Competing for ad placements and keywords in search engine marketing can be costly and competitive.

2. **Rapidly Changing Trends:**

   - **Disadvantage:** Digital marketing trends and technologies evolve quickly, requiring continuous learning and adaptation.
   - **Example:** Staying updated with algorithm changes on social media platforms and search engines can be demanding.

3. **Privacy Concerns:**

   - **Disadvantage:** Collecting and using customer data for targeted advertising can raise privacy and security concerns.
   - **Example:** Businesses must comply with data protection regulations like GDPR and manage customer data responsibly.

4. **Dependence on Technology:**

   - **Disadvantage:** Digital marketing relies heavily on technology, making businesses vulnerable to technical issues and cybersecurity threats.
   - **Example:** Website downtime or security breaches can disrupt online marketing efforts and damage brand reputation.

5. **Content Saturation:**

   - **Disadvantage:** The abundance of online content can make it challenging to capture and retain audience attention.
   - **Example:** Creating unique and engaging content that stands out among competitors requires creativity and effort.

6. **Ad Blockers:**

   - **Disadvantage:** The use of ad blockers by consumers can reduce the effectiveness of online advertising campaigns.
   - **Example:** Display ads and pop-up ads may be blocked, limiting their reach to the intended audience.

7. **Skill and Resource Requirements:**

   - **Disadvantage:** Effective digital marketing requires specialized skills and resources, which may be a barrier for small businesses.
   - **Example:** Developing and executing successful SEO, PPC, and social media campaigns often requires expertise and investment.

Conclusion

Digital marketing offers numerous benefits, including global reach, targeted advertising, cost-effectiveness, and measurable results. However, it also presents challenges such as intense competition, rapidly changing trends, privacy concerns, and dependence on technology. By understanding both the advantages and disadvantages, businesses can develop effective digital marketing strategies that capitalize on the opportunities while mitigating the risks.

CHAPTER THIRTY-TWO

E-MARKETING

E-Marketing, also known as electronic marketing or online marketing, refers to the use of digital technologies and the internet to promote products, services, and brands. It encompasses a wide range of online marketing activities aimed at reaching and engaging customers through various digital channels.

Types of E-Marketing

1. **Search Engine Optimization (SEO):**

   - **Definition:** The process of optimizing a website to rank higher in search engine results pages (SERPs) to increase organic traffic.
   - **Example:** Improving website content and structure to rank higher on Google search results.

2. **Content Marketing:**

   - **Definition:** Creating and sharing valuable, relevant, and consistent content to attract and retain a clearly defined audience.
   - **Example:** Blog posts, articles, videos, infographics, and e-books.

3. **Social Media Marketing:**

   - **Definition:** Using social media platforms to promote products, services, and brands, engage with customers, and build a community.
   - **Example:** Marketing campaigns on Facebook, Instagram, Twitter, and LinkedIn.

4. **Email Marketing:**

   - **Definition:** Sending targeted and personalized emails to a list of subscribers to promote products, share information, and build relationships.
   - **Example:** Newsletters, promotional offers, and customer surveys.

5. **Pay-Per-Click (PPC) Advertising:**

   - **Definition:** A model of online advertising where advertisers pay a fee each time their ad is clicked.
   - **Example:** Google Ads and social media ads.

6. **Affiliate Marketing:**

   - **Definition:** Partnering with affiliates who promote products and earn a commission for each sale or lead generated through their referral.
   - **Example:** Influencers or bloggers promoting products and earning a commission.

7. **Influencer Marketing:**

   - **Definition:** Collaborating with influencers who have a significant following to promote products or services.
   - **Example:** Brands partnering with social media influencers to reach their audience.

8. **Mobile Marketing:**

   - **Definition:** Promoting products and services through mobile devices using SMS, MMS, mobile apps, and mobile websites.
   - **Example:** Push notifications and in-app advertisements.

Methods of E-Marketing

1. **SEO Techniques:**

- **On-Page SEO:** Optimizing website content, meta tags, and internal linking.
- **Off-Page SEO:** Building backlinks and improving domain authority.
- **Technical SEO:** Ensuring website speed, mobile-friendliness, and secure connections (HTTPS).

2. **Content Creation:**

- **Blogs and Articles:** Writing informative and engaging content on relevant topics.
- **Videos:** Creating video content for platforms like YouTube and social media.
- **Infographics:** Designing visually appealing infographics to present data and information.

3. **Social Media Engagement:**

- **Posting and Sharing:** Regularly posting content and engaging with followers.
- **Social Media Ads:** Running paid advertising campaigns on social platforms.
- **Community Building:** Creating and nurturing online communities.

4. **Email Campaigns:**

- **Segmentation:** Dividing the email list into targeted segments based on demographics and behavior.
- **Personalization:** Customizing email content to address individual subscriber needs.
- **Automation:** Using automated email sequences for drip campaigns and follow-ups.

5. **PPC Advertising:**

- **Keyword Research:** Identifying relevant keywords for ad targeting.
- **Ad Creation:** Designing compelling ad copy and visuals.
- **Bid Management:** Setting and adjusting bid amounts to optimize ad spend.

6. **Affiliate Partnerships:**

   - **Recruitment:** Identifying and recruiting potential affiliates.
   - **Commission Structure:** Defining commission rates and payment terms.
   - **Tracking:** Monitoring affiliate performance and tracking conversions.

7. **Influencer Collaborations:**

   - **Selection:** Choosing influencers whose audience aligns with the brand.
   - **Content Creation:** Collaborating on content creation and promotion.
   - **Performance Measurement:** Analyzing the impact of influencer campaigns.

8. **Mobile Marketing Techniques:**

   - **SMS Campaigns:** Sending promotional text messages to subscribers.
   - **App Marketing:** Promoting apps through app stores and in-app advertising.
   - **Location-Based Marketing:** Using geolocation data for targeted promotions.

Advantages of E-Marketing

1. **Global Reach:** E-Marketing allows businesses to reach a worldwide audience without geographic limitations.
2. **Cost-Effectiveness:** Online marketing campaigns can be more affordable than traditional marketing methods.
3. **Targeted Marketing:** E-Marketing enables precise targeting based on demographics, interests, behavior, and location.
4. **Measurable Results:** Digital marketing provides detailed analytics and metrics to track campaign performance.
5. **Flexibility and Adaptability:** Campaigns can be easily adjusted and optimized based on real-time data and feedback.
6. **Enhanced Engagement:** Direct interaction and engagement with customers through various digital channels.

7. **Higher Conversion Rates:** Personalized and targeted messaging often leads to higher conversion rates.

Disadvantages of E-Marketing

1. **Intense Competition:** The digital landscape is highly competitive, making it challenging to stand out.
2. **Privacy Concerns:** Collecting and using customer data can raise privacy and security issues.
3. **Rapidly Changing Trends:** Digital marketing trends and technologies evolve quickly, requiring continuous learning and adaptation.
4. **Dependence on Technology:** E-Marketing relies heavily on technology, making businesses vulnerable to technical issues and cybersecurity threats.
5. **Content Saturation:** The abundance of online content can make it difficult to capture and retain audience attention.
6. **Ad Blockers:** The use of ad blockers by consumers can reduce the effectiveness of online advertising campaigns.
7. **Skill and Resource Requirements:** Effective e-marketing requires specialized skills and resources, which may be a barrier for small businesses.

Conclusion

E-Marketing offers numerous benefits, including global reach, cost-effectiveness, targeted marketing, and measurable results. However, it also presents challenges such as intense competition, privacy concerns, and dependence on technology. By understanding both the advantages and disadvantages, businesses can develop effective e-marketing strategies that capitalize on the opportunities while mitigating the risks.

CHAPTER THIRTY-THREE

GREEN MARKETING

Green Marketing involves promoting products or services based on their environmental benefits. The main objectives of green marketing are:

1. **Environmental Sustainability:** Environmental sustainability involves adopting practices that protect the environment and minimize the negative impact of human activities. This includes using renewable energy sources such as solar and wind power, reducing waste by recycling and composting, and improving energy efficiency through smart practices and technology. Sustainable transportation options, such as public transit, cycling, and electric vehicles, help decrease carbon emissions. Additionally, sustainable agricultural methods, forest conservation, and water-saving techniques contribute to preserving ecosystems and natural resources. By supporting eco-friendly products and companies, individuals can make a significant difference in promoting sustainability and reducing their carbon footprints, ultimately helping to combat climate change and safeguard the planet for future generations.

2. **Consumer Awareness:** Consumer awareness is crucial in fostering a sustainable future. It involves educating consumers about how their purchasing decisions affect the environment and encouraging them to make more eco-friendly choices. This awareness can be raised through various means such as labeling products with information on their environmental impact, running campaigns that highlight the benefits of sustainable products, and promoting the importance of reducing waste and recycling.

   By understanding the carbon footprint of products, the resources used in their production, and the waste generated by their disposal, consumers can make informed choices that support environmental preservation. For instance, choosing products with minimal packaging, opting for locally sourced goods, and supporting companies that follow sustainable practices can significantly reduce one's environmental impact. Educating consumers also involves guiding them towards alternatives like reusable items, energy-efficient appliances, and organic or sustainably sourced food.

Overall, consumer awareness empowers individuals to take responsibility for their environmental impact and contributes to a collective effort towards a greener planet.

3. **Brand Differentiation:** Brand differentiation through eco-friendly products and services allows businesses to distinguish themselves in a competitive market by aligning with growing consumer concerns about the environment. By prioritizing sustainability, companies can attract a dedicated customer base that values ethical and green practices. This includes designing products with sustainable materials, using eco-friendly packaging, and obtaining green certifications that validate their environmental efforts. Transparent practices and engaging in corporate social responsibility initiatives further build consumer trust and loyalty. Ultimately, offering eco-friendly products and services not only helps companies stand out but also contributes to a more sustainable future, fostering a positive brand image and gaining a competitive edge.

4. **Regulatory Compliance:** Regulatory compliance involves adhering to environmental laws and regulations set by governing bodies to protect the environment and public health. By ensuring that their operations meet these standards, businesses can avoid potential penalties, fines, and legal consequences. This compliance not only mitigates financial risks but also enhances a company's reputation and demonstrates its commitment to sustainability. Staying updated on regulatory changes and implementing best practices for environmental management can help businesses operate responsibly, reduce their ecological footprint, and contribute to a healthier planet. In essence, regulatory compliance is a critical aspect of sustainable business operations and long-term success.

5. **Market Expansion:** Market expansion by targeting environmentally conscious consumers is a strategic approach for businesses looking to grow. This demographic is increasingly prioritizing sustainability in their purchasing decisions, seeking out brands that reflect their values. By

offering eco-friendly products and services, companies can attract these customers and build brand loyalty. This includes incorporating sustainable materials, reducing carbon footprints, and promoting transparent and ethical practices. Aligning with environmental values not only opens up new market opportunities but also enhances the company's reputation and fosters long-term customer relationships. In essence, tapping into this growing market supports both business growth and environmental preservation.

6. **Corporate Social Responsibility:** Corporate Social Responsibility (CSR) is a critical aspect of modern business practices, focusing on a company's commitment to sustainable development and ethical conduct. CSR initiatives demonstrate that a company values more than just profit—they prioritize the well-being of the environment, communities, and society at large. This commitment is evident through various actions such as reducing environmental impacts, supporting fair labor practices, and engaging in philanthropy.

    By investing in sustainable development, companies can implement eco-friendly practices, like reducing carbon emissions and conserving natural resources, which contribute to long-term environmental health. Ethical conduct involves transparency, integrity, and accountability in business operations, ensuring that companies uphold high standards in all aspects of their work.

    Moreover, CSR initiatives often include community engagement, where businesses give back through volunteering, charitable donations, and supporting local projects. This not only enhances the company's reputation but also fosters a positive relationship with stakeholders, including customers, employees, and investors.

Evolution
Green marketing has evolved significantly over the decades:

1. **1970s:** Emergence of environmental consciousness, leading to the first wave of green marketing.
2. **1980s:** Increased focus on recycling and pollution reduction. Companies began to adopt greener practices.
3. **1990s:** Introduction of eco-labeling and certifications to identify environmentally friendly products.

4. **2000s:** Growth in consumer demand for sustainable products, leading to more comprehensive green marketing strategies.
5. **2010s:** Integration of sustainability into corporate strategies, with companies reporting on their environmental impact.
6. **2020s:** Enhanced focus on circular economy principles, zero-waste initiatives, and carbon neutrality.

Reasons for Green Marketing

1. **Consumer Demand:** Increasing consumer preference for eco-friendly products.
2. **Competitive Advantage:** Differentiating from competitors through sustainable practices.
3. **Regulatory Pressure:** Compliance with environmental regulations and standards.
4. **Cost Savings:** Reducing waste and improving resource efficiency can lower costs.
5. **Brand Image:** Enhancing brand reputation and loyalty through sustainable practices.
6. **Social Responsibility:** Fulfilling corporate social responsibility and contributing to environmental preservation.

Strategies

1. **Product Innovation:** Developing new eco-friendly products or improving existing ones to reduce their environmental impact.
2. **Eco-Labeling and Certifications:** Obtaining certifications and labels that signify environmental sustainability.
3. **Sustainable Packaging:** Using recyclable, biodegradable, or minimal packaging to reduce waste.
4. **Green Advertising:** Promoting the environmental benefits of products through marketing campaigns.
5. **Energy Efficiency:** Implementing energy-saving measures in production and operations.
6. **Corporate Transparency:** Reporting on sustainability efforts and environmental impact in corporate communications.

Impacts

1. **Environmental Benefits:** Reduction in pollution, waste, and carbon emissions, contributing to a healthier planet.
2. **Consumer Behavior:** Shifts in consumer purchasing decisions toward more sustainable products.
3. **Business Growth:** Increased market share and revenue from eco-friendly products.
4. **Brand Loyalty:** Enhanced brand loyalty and trust among environmentally conscious consumers.
5. **Regulatory Compliance:** Meeting legal requirements and avoiding penalties related to environmental regulations.

Challenges

1. **Greenwashing:** Misleading claims about the environmental benefits of products can erode consumer trust.
2. **Higher Costs:** Initial investment in sustainable practices and technologies can be high.
3. **Consumer Skepticism:** Overcoming skepticism and convincing consumers of the genuine environmental benefits of products.
4. **Market Competition:** Competing with traditional products that may be cheaper and more established.
5. **Technological Limitations:** Challenges in developing and adopting new sustainable technologies.
6. **Regulatory Complexity:** Navigating complex and varying environmental regulations across different markets.

Conclusion

Green marketing is a vital approach that aligns business practices with environmental sustainability, meeting consumer demand for eco-friendly products while supporting long-term corporate growth. Despite its challenges, the benefits of green marketing, including enhanced brand image, regulatory compliance, and positive environmental impact, make it a compelling strategy for forward-thinking companies.

CHAPTER THIRTY-FOUR

APPENDIX A: REVIEW QUESTIONS

Here are some review questions that can help you consolidate your understanding:

Marketing Information System (MIS)

1. Define a Marketing Information System (MIS) and explain its main components.
2. What are the advantages of implementing an MIS in an organization?
3. How does an MIS help in achieving organizational objectives?

Marketing Mix: Product

1. What are the key characteristics of a product in the marketing mix?
2. Explain the differences between convenience products, shopping products, specialty products, and unsought products.
3. Describe the unique characteristics of services as products.

Product Development

1. Outline the steps involved in the product development process.
2. What are the main benefits of effective product development for a business?
3. How does market testing play a role in the product development process?

Pricing Strategy

1. What are the main factors influencing pricing decisions in a business?
2. Describe the process of price determination.
3. Compare and contrast cost-based pricing and value-based pricing.

Distribution Channels

1. Define the role of middlemen in the distribution process and their functions.
2. What are the key factors to consider when choosing distribution channels?
3. Explain the different types of channel conflict and how they can be managed.

Retailers

1. What are the main functions of retailers in the distribution channel?
2. Compare the advantages and disadvantages of small-scale and large-scale retail businesses.
3. Describe the different types of retail institutions.

Sales Promotion

1. What are the main objectives of sales promotion?
2. Discuss the various promotional methods and their effectiveness.
3. What are the steps involved in planning a sales promotion campaign?

Advertising

1. Define advertising and explain its key features.
2. What are the advantages and importance of advertising in marketing?
3. List and describe the different kinds of advertising media.

Personal Selling

1. What are the key characteristics and benefits of personal selling?
2. Discuss the main steps and methods involved in personal selling.
3. What are the arguments against personal selling?

Digital Marketing

1. What are the main benefits of digital marketing for businesses?
2. Explain the disadvantages and challenges associated with digital marketing.
3. How does digital marketing differ from traditional marketing?

E-Marketing

1. Define e-marketing and describe its main types.
2. What are the advantages and disadvantages of e-marketing?
3. Discuss the various methods used in e-marketing.

Green Marketing

1. What are the main objectives of green marketing?
2. Explain the evolution of green marketing over the decades.
3. What are the challenges businesses face in implementing green marketing strategies?

Feel free to use these questions to review and deepen your understanding of each topic.